THE
JESUS BIBLE

Published by

onyourgates.com

6539 Noffke Dr.
Caledonia, Michigan 49316
Marie@onyourgates.com
(616) 893-4880
www.onyourgates.com

Other personalized books in this Bible series:

The 6 Day Bible Tract

The John Bible

The Luke Bible

The 30 Second Bible

The Jesus Bible

The Sampler Bible

The New Testament Bible

All of these Bibles can be printed with your cover, your info, and a unique message for your unique church or ministry.

The Jesus Bible
By Steven Elzinga
Copyright 2013 by Onyourgates

All rights reserved. No portion of this publication may be reproduced by any means without prior permission from the publisher: Onyourgates, 6539 Noffke Dr. Caledonia, MI 49316.

The ESV® Bible (The Holy Bible, English Standard Version®) copyright © 2001 by Crossway, a publishing ministry of Good News Publishers. ESV® Text Edition: 2011. The ESV® text has been reproduced in cooperation with and by permission of Good News Publishers. Unauthorized reproduction of this publication is prohibited. All rights reserved.

THE HOLY BIBLE, NEW INTERNATIONAL VERSION®, NIV® Copyright © 1973, 1978, 1984, 2011 by Biblica, Inc.™ Used by permission. All rights reserved worldwide.

Scripture quotations taken from the New American Standard Bible®, Copyright © 1960, 1962, 1963, 1968, 1971, 1972, 1973, 1975, 1977, 1995 by The Lockman Foundation. Used by permission. (www.Lockman.org)

Scripture quotations marked (NLT) are taken from the Holy Bible, New Living Translation, Copyright © 1996, 2004, 2007 by Tyndale House Foundation. Used by permission of Tyndale House Publishers, Inc., Carol Stream, Illinois 60188. All rights reserved.

New Revised Standard Version Bible, Copyright 1989, Division of Christian Education of the National Council of the Churches of Christ in the United States of America. Use by permission. All rights reserved.

Who is Jesus and why should you bother reading about Him?

1. His book, the Bible, has been the number one bestseller since the invention of the printing press.

2. He is the most well known man in human history.

3. More people claim to follow His teachings than the teachings of any other teacher.

4. More art and music has been inspired by Him than by anyone else.

5. Most of the humanitarian aid ministered to people in the world today is in His name.

6. Millions of volunteers, all around the world—through churches, schools, and non-profit organizations—spend millions and millions of hours and dollars trying to help people get a better life in His name.

7. Jesus is arguably the most interesting person who ever lived.

8. Jesus said and did some of the most outrageous and shocking things ever said or done.

9. Jesus claims to be the son of God who came into the world to set people free from misery and death.

10. Jesus promised more to those who trust Him than any other has ever dared to promise.

What is the Jesus Bible and why should you bother reading it?

The whole Bible—from beginning to its end—is about Jesus. His story, the thirty-three years He lived on this earth as a walking, eating, breathing man, is told in just four books—four of the sixty-six books that we call The Bible.

The first of these four books was written by Matthew, a Jew, a tax collector (hated by his own people, the lowest of the low). He became a follower of Jesus and witnessed, firsthand, what Jesus did and said throughout most of His earthly ministry. Matthew tells the story of Jesus from a Jewish perspective (so there are many quotes from the Old Testament).

The second book was written by Mark, a companion to Paul on some of his missionary journeys. (The story of Paul is found in the book of Acts; it is the story of the beginning of the church.) Mark tells the Jesus story emphasizing Him as the mighty miracle worker.

The third book was written by Luke, a physician

who also accompanied Paul on some missionary journeys. Luke emphasizes Jesus' concern for the poor, the weak, and those who knew they needed a savior.

The last book was written by John, one of the twelve disciples of Jesus and the last to die, exiled to the Greek island of Patmos.

The four tell the one story of Jesus—sometimes they tell the same story from different perspectives and sometimes they tell something unique to their own experience of Jesus.

It can be confusing—four tellings of the same story. The Jesus Bible takes all four accounts and combines them into one seamless story.

One story; four storytellers. To help keep each of the four voices distinct, the Jesus Bible assigns one version of the Bible to each of the four authors. Matthew's contribution to the Jesus Bible will be the New Revised Standard Version (NRSV). Mark, the New Living Translation (NLT). Luke, the New American Standard Bible (NASB). John, the New International Version (NIV).

After you have read the story of Jesus as told in Part One of the Jesus Bible (a harmony of the four gospels) read in Part Two how Jesus shows up in every single book of the Bible. (Part Two of the Jesus Bible will be the English Standard Version, ESV). You will be surprised and amazed at the Jesus predictions, the Jesus connections, and the Jesus prophecies that you will encounter in every book of the Bible, from Genesis to Revelation.

This is the Jesus Bible!

Many in our world have a lot to say about Jesus—good and bad. But why not read His story for yourself, first as told by those who knew Him best and then from the witness of every single author of every single book in the Bible.

Contents

Part One: Jesus in the Four Gospels

1. The Coming of Jesus (His Ministry Begins) — 4
2. The Teaching Ministry of Jesus
   - Event-based — 16
   - His Sayings — 28
   - The 7 "I Am" Sayings — 37
   - Other Sayings — 45
   - The Parables — 49
3. The Miracles of Jesus — 64
4. The Plot to Kill Jesus — 73
5. The Death of Jesus — 89
   - The 7 Words of the Cross — 89
   - The Story Continues — 92
6. The Resurrection of Jesus — 95
7. The Great Commission of Jesus — 103

Part Two: Jesus in the Rest of the Bible

1. The 5 Books of Moses — 107
2. The 12 Historical Books — 110
3. The 5 Poetic Books — 116
4. The 5 Major Prophets — 119
5. The 12 Minor Prophets — 129
6. The 4 Gospels — 137
7. The Book of Acts — 137
8. The Letters — 138
9. The Book of Revelation — 145

Part One:
Jesus in the Four Gospels

Jesus in the Four Gospels

Theme: Story of Jesus

Authors: Matthew (the tax collector called by Jesus to be a disciple), Mark (companion of Paul on a few mission trips), Luke (the physician who also accompanied Paul on several trips), John (Jesus' beloved disciple).

Location: Israel

Date: A.D. 0-33

Summary: Matthew tells the story of Jesus from a Jewish perspective (he quotes frequently from the Old Testament); Mark tells the story emphasizing Jesus as the mighty miracle-worker; Luke tells the story in an orderly way emphasizing Jesus as the teacher and friend of sinners; John tells the story with images: Jesus is the Word, the light, the door, the good shepherd, the vine, the way, the truth, and the life.

The four gospels are four different books. It will be interesting to look at them as one.

The Coming of Jesus

1. The Coming of Jesus: His Ministry Begins

In the beginning God created... Genesis 1:1

Jesus is the Word. He is God. He became a human being. He lived among us (2 Chronicles 6:18, pg. 113).

Like Sarah, Rebekah, and Hannah, and the mother of Samson in the Old Testament.

John 1:1 (NIV) **In the beginning** was the Word, and the Word was with God, and the Word was God. 2 He was with God in the beginning. 14 The **Word became flesh** and made his **dwelling** among us. We have seen his glory, the glory of the one and only Son, who came from the Father, full of grace and truth.

Birth of John the Baptist Foretold

Luke 1:5 (NASB) In the days of Herod, king of Judea, there was a priest named Zacharias, of the division of Abijah; and he had a wife from the daughters of Aaron, and her name was Elizabeth. 6 They were both righteous in the sight of God, walking blamelessly in all the commandments and requirements of the Lord. 7 But they had no child, because Elizabeth was **barren**, and they were both advanced in years.

8 Now it happened that while he was performing his priestly service before God in the appointed order of his division, 9 according to the custom of the priestly office, he was chosen by lot to enter the temple of the Lord and burn incense. 10 And the whole multitude of the people were in prayer outside at the hour of the incense offering. 11 And an angel of the Lord appeared to him, standing to the right of the altar of incense. 12 Zacharias was troubled when he saw the angel, and fear gripped him. 13 But the angel said to him, "Do not be afraid, Zacharias, for your petition has been heard, and your wife Elizabeth will bear you a son, and you will give him the name John.

14 You will have joy and gladness, and many will rejoice at his birth. 15 For he will be great in the sight of the Lord; and he will drink no wine or liquor, and he will be filled with the Holy Spirit while yet in his mother's womb. 16 And he will turn many of the sons of Israel back to the Lord their God. 17 It is he who will go as a forerunner before Him in the spirit and power of **Elijah**, to turn the hearts of the fathers back to the children, and the disobedient to the attitude of the righteous, so as to make ready a people prepared for the Lord."

18 Zacharias said to the angel, "How will I know this for certain? For I am an **old man** and my wife is **advanced in years**."

19 The angel answered and said to him, "I am Gabriel, who stands in the presence of God, and I have been sent to speak to you and to bring you this good news. 20 And behold, you shall be silent and unable to speak until the day when these things take place, because you did not believe my words, which will be fulfilled in their proper time."

21 The people were waiting for Zacharias, and were wondering at his delay in the temple. 22 But when he came out, he was unable to speak to them; and they realized that he had seen a vision in the temple; and he kept making signs to them, and remained mute. 23 When the days of his priestly service were ended, he went back home.

24 After these days Elizabeth his wife became pregnant, and she kept herself in seclusion for five months, saying, 25 "This is the way the Lord has dealt with me in the days

---

Elijah - a great prophet in the Old Testament - never died. Many thought he would come back and usher in some great event.

Like Abraham and Sarah.

The Coming of Jesus

when He looked with favor upon me, to take away my disgrace among men."

Jesus' Birth Foretold

26 Now in the sixth month the angel Gabriel was sent from God to a city in Galilee called Nazareth, 27 to a virgin engaged to a man whose name was Joseph, of the descendants of David; and the virgin's name was Mary. 28 And coming in, he said to her, "Greetings, favored one! The Lord is with you."

29 But she was very perplexed at this statement, and kept pondering what kind of salutation this was. 30 The angel said to her, "Do not be afraid, Mary; for you have found favor with God. 31 And behold, you will conceive in your womb and bear a son, and you shall name Him Jesus. 32 He will be great and will be called the Son of the Most High; and the Lord God will give Him the throne of His father David; 33 and He will reign over the house of Jacob forever, and His kingdom will have no end."

34 Mary said to the angel, "How can this be, since *I am a virgin*?"

35 The angel answered and said to her, "The Holy Spirit will come upon you, and the power of the Most High will overshadow you; and for that reason the holy Child shall be called the Son of God. 36 And behold, even your relative Elizabeth has also conceived a son in her old age; and she who was called barren is now in her sixth month. 37 For nothing will be ***impossible*** with God."

38 And Mary said, "**Behold, the bondslave**

The virgin birth was predicted hundreds of years before (Isaiah 7:14).

What impossible things do I face today?

of the Lord; may it be done to me according to your word." And the angel departed from her.

Mary Visits Elizabeth

39 Now at this time Mary arose and went in a hurry to the hill country, to a city of Judah, 40 and entered the house of Zacharias and greeted Elizabeth. 41 When Elizabeth heard Mary's greeting, the baby leaped in her womb; and Elizabeth was filled with the Holy Spirit. 42 And she cried out with a loud voice and said, "Blessed are you among women, and blessed is the fruit of your womb! 43 And how has it happened to me, that the mother of my Lord would come to me? 44 For behold, when the sound of your greeting reached my ears, the baby leaped in my womb for joy. 45 And blessed is she who believed that there would be a fulfillment of what had been spoken to her by the Lord."

The Magnificat

46 And Mary said: "My soul exalts the Lord, 47 And my spirit has rejoiced in God my Savior. 48 "For He has had regard for the humble state of His bondslave; For behold, from this time on all generations will count me blessed. 49 "***For the Mighty One has done great things for me***; And holy is His name. 50 and His mercy is upon generation after generation toward those who fear Him."

The Birth of Jesus the Messiah

Matthew 1:18 (NRSV) Now the birth of Jesus the Messiah took place in this way. When his

> Am I ready to pray these words?

> I wonder ... will God, the Mighty One, do good great things for me in my life?

The Coming of Jesus

I can't imagine trying to explain this to my parents.

Isaiah 7:14 pg. 119.

mother Mary had been engaged to Joseph, but before they lived together, **she was found to be with child from the Holy Spirit**. 19 Her husband Joseph, being a righteous man and unwilling to expose her to public disgrace, planned to dismiss her quietly. 20 But just when he had resolved to do this, an angel of the Lord appeared to him in a dream and said, "Joseph, son of David, do not be afraid to take Mary as your wife, for the child conceived in her is from the Holy Spirit. 21 She will bear a son, and you are to name him Jesus, for he will save his people from their sins." 22 All this took place to fulfill what had been spoken by the Lord through the prophet:

23 "Look, the **virgin shall conceive** and bear a son, and they shall name him Emmanuel," which means, "God is with us." 24 When Joseph awoke from sleep, he did as the angel of the Lord commanded him; he took her as his wife, 25 but had no marital relations with her until she had borne a son; and he named him Jesus.

Jesus' Birth in Bethlehem

Luke 2:1 (NASB) Now in those days a decree went out from Caesar Augustus, that a census be taken of all the inhabited earth. 2 This was the first census taken while Quirinius was governor of Syria. 3 And everyone was on his way to register for the census, each to his own city. 4 Joseph also went up from Galilee, from the city of Nazareth, to Judea, to the city of David which is called Bethlehem, because he was of the house and family of David, 5 in order to register along with Mary, who was engaged to him, and was with child. 6 While they were there, the days were completed for her to give birth. 7 And she gave birth to her firstborn son; and she wrapped Him in cloths, and laid Him in a manger, because there was **no room** for them in the inn.

8 In the same region there were some **shepherds** staying out in the fields and keeping watch over their flock by night. 9 And an angel of the Lord suddenly stood before them, and the glory of the Lord shone around them; and they were terribly frightened. 10 But the angel said to them, "Do not be afraid; for behold, I bring you good news of great joy which will be for all the people; 11 for today in the city of David there has been born for you a Savior, who is Christ the Lord. 12 This will be a sign for you: you will find a baby wrapped in cloths and lying in a manger." 13 And suddenly there appeared with the angel a multitude of the heavenly host praising God and saying, 14 "Glory to God in the highest, And on earth **peace** among men with whom He is pleased." 15 When the angels had gone away from them into heaven, the shepherds began saying to one another, "Let us go straight to Bethlehem then, and see this thing that has happened which the Lord has made known to us." 16 So they came in a hurry and found their way to Mary and Joseph, and the baby as He lay in the manger. 17 When they had seen this, they made known the statement which had been told them about this Child. 18 And all who heard it wondered at the things which were told them by the shepherds. 19 But Mary treasured all these things, pondering them in her

---

Am I making room for Jesus in my life?

Shepherds were often the poor, the young, and the marginalized. I wonder why they were the first to hear of Jesus' birth.

Isaiah 9:6, pg. 119.

The Coming of Jesus

heart. 20 The shepherds went back, glorifying and praising God for all that they had heard and seen, just as had been told them.

Jesus Presented at the Temple

21 And when eight days had passed, before His **circumcision**, His name was then called Jesus, the name given by the angel before He was conceived in the womb.

The sign of being dedicated to God.

22 And when the days for their purification according to the law of Moses were completed, they brought Him up to Jerusalem to present Him to the Lord 23 (as it is written in the Law of the Lord, "every firstborn male that opens the womb shall be called holy to the Lord"), 24 and to offer a sacrifice according to what was said in the Law of the Lord, "**A pair of turtledoves or two young pigeons**."

This was the offering of the poor. Does this mean Jesus was from a poor family? If so, I wonder what that means.

25 And there was a man in Jerusalem whose name was Simeon; and this man was righteous and devout, looking for the consolation of Israel; and the Holy Spirit was upon him. 26 And it had been revealed to him by the Holy Spirit that he would not see death before he had seen the Lord's Christ. 27 And he came in the Spirit into the temple; and when the parents brought in the child Jesus, to carry out for Him the custom of the Law, 28 then he took Him into his arms, and blessed God, and said,

29 "Now Lord, You are releasing Your bond-servant to depart in peace, According to Your word; 30 For my eyes have seen Your salvation, 31 which You have prepared in the presence of all peoples, 32 a light of revelation to the **gentiles**, and the glory of Your

non-Jews

people Israel."

33 And His father and mother were amazed at the things which were being said about Him. 34 And Simeon blessed them and said to Mary His mother, "Behold, this Child is appointed for the fall and rise of many in Israel, and for a sign to be opposed— 35 and *a sword will pierce even your own soul*—to the end that thoughts from many hearts may be revealed."

36 And there was a prophetess, Anna the daughter of Phanuel, of the tribe of Asher. She was advanced in years and had lived with her husband seven years after her marriage, 37 and then as a widow to the age of eighty-four. She never left the temple, serving night and day with fastings and prayers. 38 At that very moment she came up and began giving thanks to God, and continued to speak of Him to all those who were looking for the redemption of Jerusalem.

Return to Nazareth

39 When they had performed everything according to the Law of the Lord, they returned to Galilee, to their own city of Nazareth. 40 The Child continued to grow and become strong, increasing in wisdom; and the grace of God was upon Him.

The Visit of the Wise Men

Matthew 2:1 (NRSV) In the time of King Herod, after Jesus was born in Bethlehem of Judea, *wise men* from the East came to Jerusalem, 2 asking, "Where is the child who has been born king of the Jews? For we observed his star at its rising, and have come to

Mary would one day watch her son die on a cross.

The wise men were seekers. They didn't know the truth, but they were looking for it. Would the people that

The Coming of Jesus

know me say I am looking for the truth?

Predicted by the prophet Micah. Micah 5:2, pg. 133.

Gold: Jesus as King. Frankincense: Jesus as Priest. Myrrh: Jesus' burial.

From Isaiah 40:3; Also Malachi 3:1, pg 138.

pay him homage." 3 When King Herod heard this, he was frightened, and all Jerusalem with him; 4 and calling together all the chief priests and scribes of the people, he inquired of them where the Messiah was to be born. 5 They told him, "In **Bethlehem** of Judea; for so it has been written by the prophet:

7 Then Herod secretly called for the wise men and learned from them the exact time when the star had appeared. 8 Then he sent them to Bethlehem, saying, "Go and search diligently for the child; and when you have found him, bring me word so that I may also go and pay him homage." 9 When they had heard the king, they set out; and there, ahead of them, went the star that they had seen at its rising, until it stopped over the place where the child was. 10 When they saw that the star had stopped, they were overwhelmed with joy. 11 On entering the house, they saw the child with Mary his mother; and they knelt down and paid him homage. Then, opening their treasure chests, they offered him gifts of **gold**, **frankincense**, and **myrrh**. 12 And having been warned in a dream not to return to Herod, they left for their own country by another road.

John the Baptist Prepares the Way

Mark 1:1 (NLT) This is the Good News about Jesus the Messiah, the Son of God. It began 2 just **as the prophet Isaiah had written:** "Look, I am sending my messenger ahead of you, and he will prepare your way. 3 He is a voice shouting in the wilderness, 'Prepare the way for the LORD's coming! Clear the road for him!' 4 This messenger was John the Baptist.

He was in the wilderness and preached that people should be baptized to show that they had repented of their sins and turned to God to be forgiven. 5 All of Judea, including all the people of Jerusalem, went out to see and hear John. And when they confessed their sins, he baptized them in the Jordan River. 6 His clothes were woven from coarse camel hair, and he wore a leather belt around his waist. For food he ate locusts and wild honey. 7 John announced: "Someone is coming soon who is greater than I am—so much greater that I'm not even worthy to stoop down like a slave and untie the straps of his sandals. 8 I baptize you with water, but he will baptize you with the Holy Spirit!"

John Testifies About Jesus

John 1:29 (NIV) The next day John saw Jesus coming toward him and said, "Look, the **Lamb of God**, who takes away the sin of the world!

The Baptism and Temptation of Jesus

Mark 1:10 (NLT) As Jesus came up out of the water, he saw the heavens splitting apart and the Holy Spirit descending on him like a dove. 11 And a voice from heaven said, "***You are my dearly loved Son, and you bring me great joy.***"

Genealogy of Jesus

Luke 3:23 (NASB) When He began His ministry, Jesus Himself was about thirty years of age, being, as was supposed, the son of Joseph, the son of Eli.

Mark 1:12 (NLT) The Spirit then compelled

The lamb was used as a sacrifice at the first Passover, making it possible for the people of Israel to be freed from their bondage to Egypt. Exodus 12, pg 107.

Good words to hear from a father or a mother.

The Coming of Jesus

The people of Israel wandered in the desert for 40 years before they entered the promised land.

Jesus to go into the wilderness, 13 where he was tempted by Satan for **forty days**. He was out among the wild animals, and angels took care of him.

14 Later on, after John was arrested, Jesus went into Galilee, where he preached God's Good News. 15 "The time promised by God has come at last!" he announced. "The Kingdom of God is near! Repent of your sins and believe the Good News!"

The First Disciples

16 One day as Jesus was walking along the shore of the Sea of Galilee, he saw Simon and his brother Andrew throwing a net into the water, for they fished for a living. 17 Jesus called out to them, "Come, follow me, and I will show you how to fish for people!" 18 And they left their nets at once and followed him.

19 A little farther up the shore Jesus saw Zebedee's sons, James and John, in a boat repairing their nets. 20 He called them at once, and they also **followed** him, leaving their father, Zebedee, in the boat with the hired men.

What or who am I following?

Call of Levi (Matthew)

Luke 5:27 (NASB) After that He went out and noticed a **tax collector** named Levi sitting in the tax booth, and He said to him, "Follow Me." 28 And he left everything behind, and got up and began to follow Him.

A self-employed IRS man of the 1st century.

29 And Levi gave a **big reception for Him** in his house; and there was a great crowd of tax collectors and other people who were reclining at the table with them. 30 The Pharisees and

Who in my life needs to be introduced

their scribes began grumbling at His disciples, saying, "Why do you eat and drink with the tax collectors and sinners?" 31 And Jesus answered and said to them, "*It is not those who are well who need a physician, but those who are sick.* 32 I have not come to call the righteous but sinners to repentance."

Jesus Chooses the Twelve Apostles

Mark 3:13 (NLT) Afterward Jesus went up on a mountain and called out the ones he wanted to go with him. And they came to him. 14 Then **he appointed twelve** of them and called them his apostles. They were to accompany him, and he would send them out to preach, 15 giving them authority to cast out demons. 16 These are the twelve he chose: Simon (whom he named Peter), 17 James and John (the sons of Zebedee, but Jesus nicknamed them "Sons of Thunder"), 18 Andrew, Philip, Bartholomew, Matthew, Thomas, James (son of Alphaeus), Thaddaeus, Simon (the zealot), 19 Judas Iscariot (who later betrayed him).

to Jesus?

Good point!

Just like the 12 tribes of Israel.

2. The Teaching Ministry of Jesus: Event-based

Jesus Teaches Nicodemus

A religious lawyer

John 3:1 (NIV) Now there was a **Pharisee**, a man named Nicodemus who was a member of the Jewish ruling council. 2 He came to Jesus at night and said, "Rabbi, we know that you are a teacher who has come from God. For no one could perform the signs you are doing if God were not with him."

3 Jesus replied, "Very truly I tell you, no one can see the kingdom of God unless they are born again."

4 "How can someone be born when they are old?" Nicodemus asked. "Surely they cannot enter a second time into their mother's womb to be born!"

5 Jesus answered, "Very truly I tell you, no one can enter the kingdom of God unless they are born of water and the Spirit. 6 Flesh gives birth to flesh, but the Spirit gives birth to spirit. 7 You should not be surprised at my saying, 'You must be born again.' 8 The wind blows wherever it pleases. You hear its sound, but you cannot tell where it comes from or where it is going. So it is with everyone born of the Spirit."

9 "How can this be?" Nicodemus asked.

10 "You are Israel's teacher," said Jesus, "and do you not understand these things? 11 Very truly I tell you, we speak of what we know, and we testify to what we have seen, but still you people do not accept our testimony. 12 I

have spoken to you of earthly things and you do not believe; how then will you believe if I speak of heavenly things? 13 No one has ever gone into heaven except the one who came from heaven—the Son of Man. 14 Just as Moses lifted up the snake in the wilderness, so the **Son of Man must be lifted up**, 15 that everyone who believes may have eternal life in him."

16 "**For God so loved the world that he gave his one and only Son, that whoever believes in him shall not perish but have eternal life.** 17 For God did not send his Son into the world to condemn the world, but to save the world through him. 18 Whoever believes in him is not condemned, but whoever does not believe stands condemned already because they have not believed in the name of God's one and only Son. 19 This is the verdict: Light has come into the world, but people loved darkness instead of light because their deeds were evil. 20 Everyone who does evil hates the light, and will not come into the light for fear that their deeds will be exposed. 21 But whoever lives by the truth comes into the light, so that it may be seen plainly that what they have done has been done in the sight of God."

John Testifies Again About Jesus

22 After this, Jesus and his disciples went out into the Judean countryside, where he spent some time with them, and baptized. 23 Now John also was baptizing at Aenon near Salim, because there was plenty of water, and people were coming and being baptized.

Numbers 21, pg. 108.

Here it is, the most famous verse in the Bible. Someone once told me that you can make this verse personal by placing your name for the word "world."

Teaching: Event-based

24 (This was before John was put in prison.) 25 An argument developed between some of John's disciples and a certain Jew over the matter of ceremonial washing. 26 They came to John and said to him, "Rabbi, that man who was with you on the other side of the Jordan—the one you testified about—look, he is baptizing, and everyone is going to him."

27 To this John replied, "A person can receive only what is given them from heaven. 28 You yourselves can testify that I said, 'I am not the Messiah but am sent ahead of him.' 29 The bride belongs to the bridegroom. The friend who attends the bridegroom waits and listens for him, and is full of joy when he hears the bridegroom's voice. That joy is mine, and it is now complete. 30 He must become greater; I must become less."

31 The one who comes from above is above all; the one who is from the earth belongs to the earth, and speaks as one from the earth. The one who comes from heaven is above all. 32 He testifies to what he has seen and heard, but no one accepts his testimony. 33 Whoever has accepted it has certified that God is truthful. 34 For the one whom God has sent speaks the words of God, for God gives the Spirit without limit. 35 The Father loves the Son and has placed everything in his hands. 36 Whoever believes in the Son has eternal life, but whoever rejects the Son will not see life, for God's wrath remains on them.

Jesus Talks with a Samaritan Woman

John 4:5 (NIV) So he came to a town in Samaria called Sychar, near the plot of ground

Jacob had given to his son Joseph. 6 Jacob's well was there, and Jesus, tired as he was from the journey, sat down by the well. It was about noon. 7 When a Samaritan woman came to draw water, Jesus said to her, "Will you give me a drink?" 8 (His disciples had gone into the town to buy food.) 9 The Samaritan woman said to him, "You are a Jew and I am a Samaritan woman. How can you ask me for a drink?" (For Jews do not associate with Samaritans.)

10 Jesus answered her, "If you knew the gift of God and who it is that asks you for a drink, you would have asked him and he would have given you living water."

11 "Sir," the woman said, "you have nothing to draw with and the well is deep. Where can you get this living water? 12 Are you greater than our father Jacob, who gave us the well and drank from it himself, as did also his sons and his livestock?"

13 Jesus answered, "Everyone who drinks this water will be thirsty again, 14 but whoever drinks the water I give them will never thirst. Indeed, the water I give them will become in them a spring of water welling up to eternal life."

15 The woman said to him, "Sir, give me this water so that I won't get thirsty and have to keep coming here to draw water."

16 He told her, "Go, call your husband and come back."

17 "I have no husband," she replied.

Jesus said to her, "You are right when you say you have no husband. 18 The fact is, you have had five husbands, and the man you now have is not your husband. What you have just said is quite true."

19 "Sir," the woman said, "I can see that you are a prophet. 20 Our ancestors worshiped on this mountain, but you Jews claim that the place where we must worship is in Jerusalem."

21 "Woman," Jesus replied, "believe me, a time is coming when you will worship the Father neither on this mountain nor in Jerusalem. 22 You Samaritans worship what you do not know; we worship what we do know, for salvation is from the Jews. 23 Yet a time is coming and has now come when the true worshipers will worship the Father in the Spirit and in truth, for they are the kind of worshipers the Father seeks. 24 God is spirit, and his worshipers must worship in the Spirit and in truth."

25 The woman said, "I know that Messiah" (called Christ) "is coming. When he comes, he will explain everything to us."

26 Then Jesus declared, "I, the one speaking to you—I am he."

The Disciples Rejoin Jesus

27 Just then his disciples returned and were surprised to find him talking with a woman. But no one asked, "What do you want?" or "Why are you talking with her?"

28 Then, leaving her water jar, the woman went back to the town and said to the people, 29 "Come, see a man who told me everything I ever did. Could this be the Messiah?" 30 They came out of the town and made their way toward him.

31 Meanwhile his disciples urged him, "Rabbi, eat something."

32 But he said to them, "I have food to eat that you know nothing about."

33 Then his disciples said to each other, "Could someone have brought him food?"

34 "My food," said Jesus, "is to do the will of him who sent me and to finish his work. 35 Don't you have a saying, 'It's still four months until harvest'? I tell you, open your eyes and look at the fields! They are ripe for harvest. 36 Even now the one who reaps draws a wage and harvests a crop for eternal life, so that the sower and the reaper may be glad together. 37 Thus the saying 'One sows and another reaps' is true. 38 I sent you to reap what you have not worked for. Others have done the hard work, and you have reaped the benefits of their labor."

Many Samaritans Believe

39 Many of the Samaritans from that town believed in him because of the woman's testimony, "He told me everything I ever did." 40 So when the Samaritans came to him, they urged him to stay with them, and he stayed two days. 41 And because of his words many more became believers.

42 They said to the woman, "We no longer believe just because of what you said; now we have **heard for ourselves**, and we know that this man really is the Savior of the world."

Jesus Rejected at Nazareth

Luke 4:16 (NASB) And He came to Nazareth, where He had been brought up; and as was

It would seem people need to experience Jesus in some way before they recognize Him as the Savior.

Teaching: Event-based

His custom, He entered the synagogue on the Sabbath, and stood up to read. 17 And the book of the prophet Isaiah was handed to Him. And He opened the book and found the place where it was written,

18 "The spirit of the Lord is upon me, because he anointed me to preach the gospel to the poor. He has sent me to proclaim release to the captives, and recovery of sight to the blind, to set free those who are oppressed, 19 to proclaim the favorable year of the Lord."

20 And He closed the book, gave it back to the attendant and sat down; and the eyes of all in the synagogue were fixed on Him. 21 And He began to say to them, "Today this Scripture has been fulfilled in your hearing." 22 And all were speaking well of Him, and wondering at the gracious words which were falling from His lips; and they were saying, "Is this not Joseph's son?" 23 And He said to them, "No doubt you will quote this proverb to Me, 'Physician, heal yourself! **Whatever we heard was done at Capernaum, do here in your hometown as well.**'" 24 And He said, "Truly I say to you, no prophet is welcome in his hometown. 25 But I say to you in truth, there were many widows in Israel in the days of Elijah, when the sky was shut up for three years and six months, when a great famine came over all the land; 26 and yet Elijah was sent to none of them, but only to **Zarephath**, in the land of Sidon, to a woman who was a widow. 27 And there were many lepers in Israel in the time of Elisha the prophet; and none of them was cleansed, but only **Naaman the Syrian**." 28 And all the people in the synagogue were filled with rage

---

Jesus had healed many in Capernaum and many were disappointed that He didn't do the same in his hometown.

non-Jews

as they heard these things; 29 and they got up and drove Him out of the city, and led Him to the brow of the hill on which their city had been built, in order to throw Him down the cliff. 30 But passing through their midst, He went His way.

Luke 7:36 (NASB) Now one of the Pharisees was requesting Him to dine with him, and He entered the Pharisee's house and reclined at the table. 37 And there was a woman in the city who was a sinner; and when she learned that He was reclining at the table in the Pharisee's house, she brought an alabaster vial of perfume, 38 and standing behind Him at His feet, weeping, she began to wet His feet with her tears, and kept wiping them with the hair of her head, and kissing His feet and anointing them with the perfume. 39 Now when the Pharisee who had invited Him saw this, he said to himself, "If this man were a prophet He would know who and what sort of person this woman is who is touching Him, that she is a sinner."

Parable of Two Debtors

40 And **Jesus answered him**, "Simon, I have something to say to you." And he replied, "Say it, Teacher." 41 "A moneylender had two debtors: one owed five hundred denarii, and the other fifty. 42 When they were unable to repay, he graciously forgave them both. So which of them will love him more?" 43 Simon answered and said, "I suppose the one whom he forgave more." And He said to him, "You have judged correctly." 44 Turning toward the woman, He said to Simon, "Do you see this

Jesus answered him thus proving to Simon that he was indeed a prophet.

Teaching: Event-based

woman? I entered your house; you gave Me no water for My feet, but she has wet My feet with her tears and wiped them with her hair. 45 You gave Me no kiss; but she, since the time I came in, has not ceased to kiss My feet. 46 You did not anoint My head with oil, but she anointed My feet with perfume. 47 For this reason I say to you, her sins, which are many, have been forgiven, for she loved much; but he who is forgiven little, loves little." 48 Then He said to her, "Your sins have been forgiven." 49 Those who were reclining at the table with Him began to say to themselves, "Who is this man who even forgives sins?" 50 And He said to the woman, "Your faith has saved you; go in peace."

The Harvest Is Great, the Laborers Few

Matthew 9:35 (NRSV) Then Jesus went about all the cities and villages, teaching in their synagogues, and proclaiming the good news of the kingdom, and curing every disease and every sickness. 36 When he saw the crowds, he had compassion for them, because they were harassed and helpless, like **sheep without a shepherd**. 37 Then he said to his disciples, "The harvest is plentiful, but the laborers are few; 38 therefore ask the Lord of the harvest to send out laborers into his harvest."

> It is easy to feel lost in a world with so many choices.

True Greatness

Matthew 18:1 (NRSV) At that time the disciples came to Jesus and asked, "Who is the greatest in the kingdom of heaven?" 2 He called a child, whom he put among them, 3 and said, "Truly I tell you, unless you change and become like children, you will never enter the kingdom of heaven. 4 Whoever becomes humble like this child is the greatest in the kingdom of heaven. 5 Whoever welcomes one such child in my name welcomes me.

Temptations to Sin

6 "If any of you put a stumbling block before one of these little ones who believe in me, it would be better for you if a great millstone were fastened around your neck and you were drowned in the depth of the sea."

The Rich Young Man

Matthew 19:16 (NRSV) Then someone came to him and said, "Teacher, what good deed must I do to have eternal life?" 17 And he said to him, "Why do you ask me about what is good? There is only one who is good. If you wish to enter into life, keep the commandments." 18 He said to him, "Which ones?" And Jesus said, "You shall not murder; You shall not commit adultery; You shall not steal; You shall not bear false witness; 19 Honor your father and mother; also, You shall love your neighbor as yourself." 20 The young man said to him, "I have kept all these; what do I still lack?" 21 Jesus said to him, "If you wish to be perfect, go, sell your possessions, and give the money to the poor, and you will have treasure in heaven; then come, follow me." 22 When the young man heard this word, he went away grieving, for he had many possessions.

23 Then Jesus said to his disciples, "Truly I tell you, it will be hard for a rich person to enter

Teaching: Event-based

the kingdom of heaven. 24 Again I tell you, it is easier for a camel to go through the eye of a needle than for someone who is rich to enter the kingdom of God." 25 When the disciples heard this, they were greatly astounded and said, "Then who can be saved?" 26 But Jesus looked at them and said, "For mortals it is impossible, but for God all things are possible."

27 Then Peter said in reply, "Look, we have left everything and followed you. What then will we have?" 28 Jesus said to them, "Truly I tell you, at the renewal of all things, when the Son of Man is seated on the throne of his glory, you who have followed me will also sit on twelve thrones, judging the twelve tribes of Israel. 29 And everyone who has left houses or brothers or sisters or father or mother or children or fields, for my name's sake, will receive a hundredfold, and will inherit eternal life. 30 But many who are first will be last, and the last will be first.

Woman Caught in Adultery

John 8:3 (NIV) The teachers of the law and the Pharisees brought in a **woman caught in adultery**. They made her stand before the group 4 and said to Jesus, "Teacher, this woman was **caught in the act** of adultery. 5 In the Law Moses commanded us to stone such women. Now what do you say?" 6 They were using this question as a trap, in order to have a basis for accusing him.

But Jesus bent down and started to **write** on the ground with his finger. 7 When they kept on questioning him, he straightened up and said to them, "Let any one of you who is without sin

Margin notes:

Where was the guilty man?

The men must've been looking and watching.

I wonder what Jesus wrote?

be the first to throw a stone at her." 8 Again he stooped down and wrote on the ground.

9 At this, those who heard began to go away one at a time, the older ones first, until only Jesus was left, with the woman still standing there. 10 Jesus straightened up and asked her, "Woman, where are they? **Has no one condemned you?**"

11 "No one, sir," she said.

"Then neither do I condemn you," Jesus declared. "Go now and leave your life of sin."

Do I live in a glass house? Maybe I should stop collecting stones.

The Teaching Ministry of Jesus: His Sayings

Jesus Sermon on the Mount (Beatitudes)

Matthew 5:1 (NRSV) When Jesus saw the crowds, he went up the mountain; and after he sat down, his disciples came to him. 2 Then he began to speak, and taught them, saying:

3 "Blessed are the poor in spirit, for theirs is the kingdom of heaven." 4 "Blessed are those who mourn, for they will be comforted." 5 "Blessed are the meek, for they will inherit the earth." 6 "Blessed are those who hunger and thirst for righteousness, for they will be filled." 7 "Blessed are the merciful, for they will receive mercy." 8 "Blessed are the pure in heart, for they will see God." 9 "Blessed are the peacemakers, for they will be called children of God." 10 "Blessed are those who are persecuted for righteousness' sake, for theirs is the kingdom of heaven." 11 "Blessed are you when people revile you and persecute you and utter all kinds of evil against you falsely on my account. 12 Rejoice and be glad, for your reward is great in heaven, for in the same way they persecuted the prophets who were before you."

Salt and Light

13 "You are the salt of the earth; but if salt has lost its taste, how can its saltiness be restored? It is no longer good for anything, but is thrown out and trampled under foot."

14 "You are the light of the world. A city built on a hill cannot be hid. 15 No one after lighting

a lamp puts it under the bushel basket, but on the lampstand, and it gives light to all in the house. 16 In the same way, let your light shine before others, so that they may see your good works and give glory to your Father in heaven."

The Law and the Prophets

17 "Do not think that I have come to abolish the law or the prophets; I have come not to abolish but to fulfill. 18 For truly I tell you, until heaven and earth pass away, not one letter, not one stroke of a letter, will pass from the law until all is accomplished. 19 Therefore, whoever breaks one of the least of these commandments, and teaches others to do the same, will be called least in the kingdom of heaven; but whoever does them and teaches them will be called great in the kingdom of heaven. 20 For I tell you, unless your righteousness exceeds that of the **scribes** and **Pharisees**, you will never enter the kingdom of heaven."

These were the most religious people of the day.

Concerning Anger

21 "You have heard that it was said to those of ancient times, 'You shall not murder'; and 'whoever murders shall be liable to judgment.' 22 But I say to you that if you are **angry** with a brother or sister, you will be liable to judgment; and if you insult a brother or sister, you will be liable to the council; and if you say, 'You fool,' you will be liable to the hell of fire. 23 So when you are offering your gift at the altar, if you remember that your brother or sister has something against you, 24 leave your gift there before the altar and go; first be

Who am I angry with these days?

Teaching: His Sayings

reconciled to your brother or sister, and then come and offer your gift. 25 Come to terms quickly with your accuser while you are on the way to court with him, or your accuser may hand you over to the judge, and the judge to the guard, and you will be thrown into prison. 26 Truly I tell you, you will never get out until you have paid the last penny."

Concerning Adultery

27 "You have heard that it was said, 'You shall not commit adultery.' 28 But I say to you that everyone who **looks** at a woman with lust has already committed adultery with her in his heart. 29 If your right eye causes you to sin, tear it out and throw it away; it is better for you to lose one of your members than for your whole body to be thrown into hell. 30 And if your right hand causes you to sin, cut it off and throw it away; it is better for you to lose one of your members than for your whole body to go into hell."

So easy to do with the internet.

Concerning Divorce

31 "It was also said, 'Whoever divorces his wife, let him give her a certificate of divorce.' 32 But I say to you that anyone who divorces his wife, except on the ground of unchastity, causes her to commit adultery; and whoever marries a divorced woman commits adultery."

Concerning Oaths

33 "Again, you have heard that it was said to those of ancient times, 'You shall not swear falsely, but carry out the vows you have made to the Lord.' 34 But I say to you, Do not swear

at all, either by heaven, for it is the throne of God, 35 or by the earth, for it is his footstool, or by Jerusalem, for it is the city of the great King. 36 And do not swear by your head, for you cannot make one hair white or black. 37 Let your word be 'Yes, Yes' or 'No, No'; anything more than this comes from the evil one."

Concerning Retaliation

38 "You have heard that it was said, 'An eye for an eye and a tooth for a tooth.' 39 But I say to you, Do not resist an evildoer. But if anyone strikes you on the right cheek, turn the other also; 40 and if anyone wants to sue you and take your coat, give your cloak as well; 41 and if anyone forces you to go one mile, go also the second mile. 42 Give to everyone who begs from you, and do not refuse anyone who wants to borrow from you."

Love for Enemies

43 "You have heard that it was said, 'You shall love your neighbor and hate your enemy.' 44 But I say to you, **Love your enemies** and pray for those who persecute you, 45 so that you may be children of your Father in heaven; for he makes his sun rise on the evil and on the good, and sends rain on the righteous and on the unrighteous. 46 For if you love those who love you, what reward do you have? Do not even the tax collectors do the same? 47 And if you greet only your brothers and sisters, what more are you doing than others? Do not even the Gentiles do the same? 48 **Be perfect**, therefore, as your heavenly Father is perfect."

Really? Love is not what comes to mind when I think of my enemies.

Another tough word.

Teaching: His Sayings

Concerning Almsgiving

Matthew 6:1 (NRSV) "Beware of practicing your piety before others in order to be seen by them; for then you have no reward from your Father in heaven."

Alms are any gifts given to the poor.

2 "So whenever you give **alms**, do not sound a trumpet before you, as the hypocrites do in the synagogues and in the streets, so that they may be praised by others. Truly I tell you, they have received their reward. 3 But when you give alms, do not let your left hand know what your right hand is doing, 4 so that your alms may be done in secret; and your Father who sees in secret will reward you."

Concerning Prayer

5 "And whenever you pray, do not be like the hypocrites; for they love to stand and pray in the synagogues and at the street corners, so that they may be seen by others. Truly I tell you, they have received their reward. 6 But whenever you pray, go into your room and shut the door and pray to your Father who is in secret; and your Father who sees in secret will reward you."

7 "When you are praying, do not heap up empty phrases as the Gentiles do; for they think that they will be heard because of their many words. 8 Do not be like them, for your Father knows what you need before you ask him."

9 "**Pray then in this way**:

This is the Lord's Prayer. The typical

Our Father in heaven, hallowed be your name. 10 Your kingdom come. Your will be done, on earth as it is in heaven. 11 Give us this day our daily bread. 12 And forgive us our debts, as we also have forgiven our debtors. 13 And do not bring us to the time of trial, but rescue us from the evil one.

14 For if you forgive others their trespasses, your heavenly Father will also forgive you; 15 but if you do not forgive others, neither will your Father forgive your trespasses."

Concerning Fasting

16 "And whenever you fast, do not look dismal, like the hypocrites, for they disfigure their faces so as to show others that they are fasting. Truly I tell you, they have received their reward. 17 But when you fast, put oil on your head and wash your face, 18 so that your fasting may be seen not by others but by your Father who is in secret; and your Father who sees in secret will reward you."

Concerning Treasures

19 "Do not store up for yourselves treasures on earth, where moth and rust consume and where thieves break in and steal; 20 but store up for yourselves treasures in heaven, where neither moth nor rust consumes and where thieves do not break in and steal. 21 For where your **treasure** is, there your heart will be also."

The Sound Eye

22 "The eye is the lamp of the body. So, if your eye is healthy, your whole body will be full of light; 23 but if your eye is unhealthy, your whole body will be full of darkness. If then the light in you is darkness, how great is the darkness!"

---

ending: "For Thine is the Kingdom, and the power and the glory forever. Amen." isn't in the text. It was added as a way to end the prayer many years later.

Someone once told me that if you want to know what your treasure is just look at where you spend most of your time and money.

Teaching: His Sayings

But I can serve God with my wealth.

Serving Two Masters

24 "No one can serve two masters; for a slave will either hate the one and love the other, or be devoted to the one and despise the other. **You cannot serve God and wealth.**"

Do Not Worry

25 "Therefore I tell you, do not worry about your life, what you will eat or what you will drink, or about your body, what you will wear. Is not life more than food, and the body more than clothing? 26 Look at the birds of the air; they neither sow nor reap nor gather into barns, and yet your heavenly Father feeds them. Are you not of more value than they? 27 And can any of you by worrying add a single hour to your span of life? 28 And why do you worry about clothing? Consider the lilies of the field, how they grow; they neither toil nor spin, 29 yet I tell you, even Solomon in all his glory was not clothed like one of these. 30 But if God so clothes the grass of the field, which is alive today and tomorrow is thrown into the oven, will he not much more clothe you—you of little faith? 31 Therefore do not worry, saying, 'What will we eat?' or 'What will we drink?' or 'What will we wear?' 32 For it is the Gentiles who strive for all these things; and indeed your heavenly Father knows that you need all these things. 33 But strive first for the kingdom of God and his righteousness, and all these things will be given to you as well."

What am I worrying about these days?

34 "So **do not worry about tomorrow**, for tomorrow will bring worries of its own. Today's trouble is enough for today."

Judging Others

Matthew 7:1 (NRSV) "Do not judge, so that you may not be judged. 2 For with the judgment you make you will be judged, and the measure you give will be the measure you get. 3 Why do you see the **speck** in your neighbor's eye, but do not notice the log in your own eye? 4 Or how can you say to your neighbor, 'Let me take the speck out of your eye,' while the log is in your own eye? 5 You hypocrite, first take the log out of your own eye, and then you will see clearly to take the speck out of your neighbor's eye."

Makes sense. Why don't I do it this way?

Ask, Search, Knock

7 "**Ask**, and it will be given you; **search**, and you will find; **knock**, and the door will be opened for you. 8 For everyone who asks receives, and everyone who searches finds, and for everyone who knocks, the door will be opened. 9 Is there anyone among you who, if your child asks for bread, will give a stone? 10 Or if the child asks for a fish, will give a snake? 11 If you then, who are evil, know how to give good gifts to your children, how much more will your Father in heaven give good things to those who ask him!"

What questions am I asking these days?
What am seeking with my time and my money?
What doors of opportunity should I be knocking on?

The Golden Rule

12 "In everything **do to others as you would have them do to you**; for this is the law and the prophets."

The golden rule.

The Narrow Gate

13 "Enter through the narrow gate; for the gate is **wide** and the road is **easy** that to de-

It is easy just to do

Teaching: His Sayings

as everyone around me does.

struction, and there are many who take it. 14 For the gate is narrow and the road is hard that leads to life, and there are few who find it."

A Tree and Its Fruit

15 "Beware of false prophets, who come to you in sheep's clothing but inwardly are ravenous wolves. 16 You will know them by their fruits. Are grapes gathered from thorns, or figs from thistles? 17 In the same way, every good tree bears good fruit, but the bad tree bears bad fruit. 18 A good tree cannot bear bad fruit, nor can a bad tree bear good fruit. 19 Every tree that does not bear good fruit is cut down and thrown into the fire. 20 Thus **you will know them by their fruits**."

What do people think of me - based on my fruit?

Concerning Self-Deception

21 "Not everyone who says to me, 'Lord, Lord,' will enter the kingdom of heaven, but only the one who does the will of my Father in heaven. 22 On that day many will say to me, 'Lord, Lord, did we not prophesy in your name, and cast out demons in your name, and do many deeds of power in your name?' 23 Then I will declare to them, '*I never knew you*; go away from me, you evildoers.'"

Very sobering!

Hearers and Doers

28 Now when Jesus had finished saying these things, the crowds were astounded at his teaching, 29 for he taught them as one having authority, and not as their scribes.

The Teaching Ministry of Jesus: The 7 "I am" Sayings

1. "I am the Bread of Life."

John 6:32 (NIV) Jesus said to them, "Very truly I tell you, it is not **Moses** who has given you the **bread from heaven**, but it is my Father who gives you the true bread from heaven. 33 For the bread of God is the bread that comes down from heaven and gives life to the world."

34 "Sir," they said, "always give us this bread."

35 Then Jesus declared, "I am the bread of life. Whoever comes to me will never go hungry, and whoever believes in me will never be thirsty. 36 But as I told you, you have seen me and still you do not believe."

41 At this the Jews there began to grumble about him because he said, "I am the bread that came down from heaven." 42 They said, "Is this not Jesus, the son of Joseph, whose father and mother we know? How can he now say, 'I came down from heaven'?"

43 "Stop grumbling among yourselves," Jesus answered. 44 "No one can come to me unless the Father who sent me draws them, and I will raise them up at the last day. 45 It is written in the Prophets: 'They will all be taught by God.' Everyone who has heard the Father and learned from him comes to me. 46 No one has seen the Father except the one who is from God; only he has seen the Father. 47 Very truly I tell you, the one who believes has eternal life. 48 I am the bread of life. 49 Your ancestors ate the manna in the wilderness, yet

The bread from heaven (manna as it was called) miraculously fell from the sky to feed the people of Israel in the desert. Exodus 16:14,15; pg.108.

Teaching: The 7 "I am" Sayings

they died. 50 But here is the bread that comes down from heaven, which anyone may eat and not die. 51 I am the living bread that came down from heaven. Whoever eats this bread will live forever. This bread is my flesh, which I will give for the life of the world."

52 Then the Jews began to argue sharply among themselves, "How can this man give us his flesh to eat?"

53 Jesus said to them, "Very truly I tell you, unless you eat the flesh of the Son of Man and drink his blood, you have no life in you. 54 Whoever eats my flesh and drinks my blood has eternal life, and I will raise them up at the last day. 55 For my flesh is real food and my blood is real drink. 56 Whoever eats my flesh and drinks my blood remains in me, and I in them. 57 Just as the living Father sent me and I live because of the Father, so the one who feeds on me will live because of me. 58 This is the bread that came down from heaven. Your ancestors ate manna and died, but whoever feeds on this bread will live forever." 59 He said this while teaching in the synagogue in Capernaum.

Many Disciples Desert Jesus

60 On hearing it, many of his disciples said, "This is a hard teaching. Who can accept it?"

61 Aware that his disciples were grumbling about this, Jesus said to them, "Does this offend you? 62 Then what if you see the Son of Man ascend to where he was before! 63 The Spirit gives life; the flesh counts for nothing. The words I have spoken to you—they are full

of the Spirit and life. 64 Yet there are some of you who do not believe." For Jesus had known from the beginning which of them did not believe and who would betray him. 65 He went on to say, "This is why I told you that no one can come to me unless the Father has enabled them."

66 From this time many of his disciples turned back and no longer followed him.

67 "You do not want to leave too, do you?" Jesus asked the Twelve.

68 **Simon Peter answered him, "Lord, to whom shall we go?** You have the words of eternal life. 69 We have come to believe and to know that you are the Holy One of God."

2. "I am the Light of the World."

Dispute over Jesus' Testimony

John 8:12 (NIV) When Jesus spoke again to the people, he said, "I am the light of the world. Whoever follows me will never walk in darkness, but will have the light of life."

Jesus Heals a Man Born Blind

John 9:1 (NIV) As he went along, he saw a man blind from birth. 2 His disciples asked him, "Rabbi, who sinned, this man or his parents, that he was born blind?"

3 "Neither this man nor his parents sinned," said Jesus, "but this happened so that the works of God might be displayed in him. 4 As long as it is day, we must do the works of him who sent me. Night is coming, when no one can work. 5 While I am in the world, I am the

---

Good question.

Good answer. If I am not going to follow Jesus, who am I going to follow?

light of the world."

John 12:44 (NIV) Then Jesus cried out, "Whoever believes in me does not believe in me only, but in the one who sent me. 45 The one who looks at me is seeing the one who sent me. 46 I have come into the world as a light, so that no one who believes in me should stay in darkness."

3. "I am the Door."

The Good Shepherd and His Sheep

John 10:1 (NIV) "Very truly I tell you Pharisees, anyone who does not enter the sheep pen by the gate, but climbs in by some other way, is a thief and a robber. 2 The one who enters by the gate is the shepherd of the sheep. 3 The gatekeeper opens the gate for him, and the sheep listen to his voice. He calls his own sheep by name and leads them out. 4 When he has brought out all his own, he goes on ahead of them, and his sheep follow him because they know his voice. 5 But they will never follow a stranger; in fact, they will run away from him because they do not recognize a stranger's voice." 6 Jesus used this figure of speech, but the Pharisees did not understand what he was telling them.

7 Therefore Jesus said again, "Very truly I tell you, I am the gate for the sheep. 8 All who have come before me are thieves and robbers, but the sheep have not listened to them. 9 I am the gate; whoever enters through me will be saved. They will come in and go out, and find pasture. 10 The thief comes only to steal and kill and destroy; I have come that they

may have life, and have it to the full."

4. "I am the Good Shepherd."

John 10:11 (NIV) "I am the good shepherd. The good shepherd lays down his life for **the sheep**. 12 The hired hand is not the shepherd and does not own the sheep. So when he sees the wolf coming, he abandons the sheep and runs away. Then the wolf attacks the flock and scatters it. 13 The man runs away because he is a hired hand and cares nothing for the sheep."

14 "I am the good shepherd; **I know my sheep and my sheep know me**— 15 just as the Father knows me and I know the Father— and **I lay down my life** for the sheep. 16 I have other sheep that are not of this sheep pen. I must bring them also. They too will listen to my voice, and there shall be one flock and one shepherd. 17 The reason my Father loves me is that I lay down my life—only to take it up again. 18 No one takes it from me, but I lay it down of my own accord. I have authority to lay it down and authority to take it up again. This command I received from my Father."

5. "I am the Resurrection and the Life."

{Lazarus, a friend of Jesus, had died and was in the grave four days when Jesus comes on the scene and talks with Martha, the sister of Lazarus.}

John 11:21 (NIV) "Lord," Martha said to Jesus, "if you had been here, my brother would not have died. 22 But I know that even now God will give you whatever you ask."

23 Jesus said to her, "Your brother will rise

Margin notes:
- Psalms 23, pg. 118.
- Ezekiel 34:31 pg. 124. On the cross.

again."

24 Martha answered, "I know he will rise again in the resurrection at the last day."

25 Jesus said to her, "I am the resurrection and the life. The one who believes in me will live, even though they die; 26 and whoever lives by believing in me will never die. **Do you believe this?**"

Do I believe this?

27 "Yes, Lord," she replied, "I believe that you are the Messiah, the Son of God, who is to come into the world."

Jesus Raises Lazarus from the Dead

38 Jesus, once more deeply moved, came to the tomb. It was a cave with a stone laid across the entrance. 39 "Take away the stone," he said.

"But, Lord," said Martha, the sister of the dead man, "by this time there is a bad odor, for he has been there four days."

40 Then Jesus said, "Did I not tell you that if you believe, you will see the glory of God?"

41 So they took away the stone. Then Jesus looked up and said, "Father, I thank you that you have heard me. 42 I knew that you always hear me, but I said this for the benefit of the people standing here, that they may believe that you sent me."

43 When he had said this, Jesus called in a loud voice, "Lazarus, come out!" 44 The dead man came out, his hands and feet wrapped with strips of linen, and a cloth around his face.

Jesus said to them, "Take off the grave

clothes and let him go."

6. "I am the Way and the Truth and the Life."

Jesus Comforts His Disciples

John 14:1 (NIV) "Do not let your hearts be troubled. You believe in God; believe also in me. 2 My Father's **house** has many rooms; if that were not so, would I have told you that I am going there to prepare a place for you? 3 And if I go and prepare a place for you, I will come back and take you to be with me that you also may be where I am. 4 You know the way to the place where I am going."

Jesus the Way to the Father

5 Thomas said to him, "Lord, we don't know where you are going, so how can we know the way?"

6 Jesus answered, "*I am the way* and the truth and the life. No one comes to the Father except through me. 7 If you really know me, you will know my Father as well. From now on, you do know him and have seen him."

7. "I am the Vine."

John 15:1 (NIV) "I am the true vine, and my Father is the gardener. 2 He cuts off every branch in me that bears no fruit, while every branch that does bear fruit he **prunes** so that it will be even more fruitful.

4 Remain in me, as I also remain in you. No branch can bear fruit by itself; it must remain in the vine. Neither can you bear fruit unless you remain in me."

5 "I am the vine; you are the branches. If you

Heaven

Jesus said that He was the way. Am I following it?

So this is what God has been doing with me lately?

Teaching: The 7 "I am" Sayings

[Margin note: What kind of fruit am I bearing?]

remain in me and I in you, you will bear much fruit; apart from me you can do nothing. 6 If you do not remain in me, you are like a branch that is thrown away and withers; such branches are picked up, thrown into the fire and burned. 7 If you remain in me and my words remain in you, ask whatever you wish, and it will be done for you. 8 This is to my Father's glory, **that you bear much fruit**, showing yourselves to be my disciples."

[Margin note: This is God's desire for me — JOY!]

9 "As the Father has loved me, so have I loved you. Now remain in my love. 10 If you keep my commands, you will remain in my love, just as I have kept my Father's commands and remain in his love. 11 I have told you this so **that my joy may be in you** and that your joy may be complete. 12 My command is this: Love each other as I have loved you. 13 Greater love has no one than this: to lay down one's life for one's friends. 14 You are my friends if you do what I command. 15 I no longer call you servants, because a servant does not know his master's business. Instead, I have called you friends, for everything that I learned from my Father I have made known to you. 16 You did not choose me, but I chose you and appointed you so that you might go and bear fruit—fruit that will last—and so that whatever you ask in my name the Father will give you."

The Teaching Ministry of Jesus: Other Sayings

Luke 11:33 (NASB) "No one, after lighting a lamp, puts it away in a cellar nor under a basket, but on the lampstand, so that those who enter may see the light. 34 The eye is the lamp of your body; when your eye is clear, your whole body also is full of light; but when it is bad, your body also is full of darkness. 35 Then watch out that the light in you is not darkness. 36 If therefore your whole body is full of light, with no dark part in it, it will be wholly illumined, as when the lamp illumines you with its rays."

Woes upon the Pharisees

37 Now when He had spoken, a Pharisee asked Him to have lunch with him; and He went in, and reclined at the table. 38 When the Pharisee saw it, he was surprised that He had not first ceremonially washed before the meal. 39 But the Lord said to him, "Now you Pharisees clean the outside of the cup and of the platter; but inside of you, you are full of robbery and wickedness. 40 You foolish ones, did not He who made the outside make the inside also? 41 But give that which is within as charity, and then all things are clean for you."

42 "But woe to you Pharisees! For you pay tithe of mint and rue and every kind of garden herb, and yet disregard justice and the love of God; but these are the things you should have done without neglecting the others. 43 Woe to you Pharisees! For you love the chief seats in the synagogues and the respectful greetings

Teaching: Other sayings

in the market places."

God Knows and Cares

Luke 12:4 (NASB) "I say to you, My friends, do not be afraid of those who kill the body and after that have no more that they can do. 5 But I will warn you whom to fear: fear the One who, after He has killed, has authority to cast into hell; yes, I tell you, fear Him! 6 Are not five sparrows sold for two cents? Yet not one of them is **forgotten** before God. 7 Indeed, the very hairs of your head are all numbered. Do not fear; you are more valuable than many sparrows."

> *Dear God, sometimes I feel alone ... and forgotten.*

8 "And I say to you, everyone who confesses Me before men, the Son of Man will confess him also before the angels of God; 9 but he who denies Me before men will be denied before the angels of God. 10 And everyone who speaks a word against the Son of Man, it will be forgiven him; but he who blasphemes against the Holy Spirit, it will not be forgiven him. 11 When they bring you before the synagogues and the rulers and the authorities, do not worry about how or what you are to speak in your defense, or what you are to say; 12 for the Holy Spirit will teach you in that very hour what you ought to say."

Covetousness Denounced

Luke 12:22 (NASB) And He said to His disciples, "For this reason I say to you, **do not worry** about your life, as to what you will eat; nor for your body, as to what you will put on. 23 For life is more than food, and the body more than clothing. 24 Consider the ravens, for

> *Easy to say!*

they neither sow nor reap; they have no storeroom nor barn, and yet God feeds them; how much more valuable you are than the birds! 25 **And which of you by worrying can add a single hour to his life's span?** 26 If then you cannot do even a very little thing, why do you worry about other matters? 27 Consider the lilies, how they grow: they neither toil nor spin; but I tell you, not even Solomon in all his glory clothed himself like one of these. 28 But if God so clothes the grass in the field, which is alive today and tomorrow is thrown into the furnace, how much more will He clothe you? You men of little faith! 29 And do not seek what you will eat and what you will drink, and do not keep worrying. 30 For all these things the nations of the world eagerly seek; but your Father knows that you need these things. 31 But seek His kingdom, and these things will be added to you. 32 Do not be afraid, little flock, for your Father has chosen gladly to give you the kingdom."

33 "Sell your possessions and give to charity; make yourselves money belts which do not wear out, an unfailing treasure in heaven, where no thief comes near nor moth destroys. 34 For where your treasure is, there your heart will be also."

Reproving Another Who Sins

Matthew 18:15 (NRSV) *"**If another member of the church sins against you, go and point out the fault when the two of you are alone**. If the member listens to you, you have regained that one. 16 But if you are not listened to, take one or two others along with

> Sometimes I worry because it is something I can do.

> This is so hard to do. It is easier to go to a sympathetic listener.

you, so that every word may be confirmed by the evidence of two or three witnesses. 17 If the member refuses to listen to them, tell it to the church; and if the offender refuses to listen even to the church, let such a one be to you as a Gentile and a tax collector."

The Teaching Ministry of Jesus: The Parables

The Parable of the Sower

Matthew 13:1 (NRSV) ... Jesus went out of the house and sat beside the sea. 2 Such great crowds gathered around him that he got into a boat and sat there, while the whole crowd stood on the beach. 3 And he told them many things in parables, saying: "Listen! A sower went out to sow. 4 And as he sowed, some seeds fell on the path, and the birds came and ate them up. 5 Other seeds fell on rocky ground, where they did not have much soil, and they sprang up quickly, since they had no depth of soil. 6 But when the sun rose, they were scorched; and since they had no root, they withered away. 7 Other seeds fell among thorns, and the thorns grew up and choked them. 8 Other seeds fell on good soil and brought forth grain, some a hundredfold, some sixty, some thirty. 9 Let anyone with ears listen!"

The Parable of the Sower Explained

18 "Hear then the parable of the sower. 19 When anyone hears the word of the kingdom and does not understand it, the evil one comes and snatches away what is sown in the heart; this is what was sown on the **path**. 20 As for what was sown on **rocky ground**, this is the one who hears the word and immediately receives it with joy; 21 yet such a person has no root, but endures only for a while, and when trouble or persecution arises on account of the word, that person immediately falls away. 22 As for what was sown among **thorns**, this is the one

I can relate parts of my

Teaching: The Parables 50

[margin note: life to all four soils.]

who hears the word, but the cares of the world and the lure of wealth choke the word, and it yields nothing. 23 But as for what was sown on **good soil**, this is the one who hears the word and understands it, who indeed bears fruit and yields, in one case a hundredfold, in another sixty, and in another thirty."

The Parable of Weeds Among the Wheat

24 He put before them another parable: "The kingdom of heaven may be compared to someone who sowed good seed in his field; 25 but while everybody was asleep, an enemy came and sowed weeds among the wheat, and then went away. 26 So when the plants came up and bore grain, then the weeds appeared as well. 27 And the slaves of the householder came and said to him, 'Master, did you not sow good seed in your field? Where, then, did these weeds come from?' 28 He answered, 'An enemy has done this.' The slaves said to him, 'Then do you want us to go and gather them?' 29 But he replied, 'No; for in gathering the weeds you would uproot the wheat along with them. 30 Let both of them grow together until the harvest; and at harvest time I will tell the reapers, Collect the weeds first and bind them in bundles to be burned, but gather the wheat into my barn.'"

The Parable of the Mustard Seed

31 He put before them another parable: "The kingdom of heaven is like a mustard seed that someone took and sowed in his field; 32 it is the smallest of all the seeds, but when it has grown it is the greatest of shrubs and be-

comes a tree, so that the birds of the air come and make nests in its branches."

The Parable of the Yeast

33 He told them another parable: "The kingdom of heaven is like yeast that a woman took and mixed in with three measures of flour until all of it was leavened."

The Use of Parables

34 Jesus told the crowds all these things in parables; without a parable he told them nothing. 35 This was to fulfill what had been spoken through the prophet:

"I will open my mouth to speak in parables; I will proclaim what has been hidden from the foundation of the world."

Jesus Explains the Parable of the Weeds

36 Then he left the crowds and went into the house. And his disciples approached him, saying, "Explain to us the parable of the weeds of the field." 37 He answered, "The one who sows the good seed is the Son of Man; 38 the field is the world, and the good seed are the children of the kingdom; the weeds are the children of the evil one, 39 and the enemy who sowed them is the devil; the harvest is the end of the age, and the reapers are angels. 40 Just as the weeds are collected and burned up with fire, so will it be at the end of the age. 41 The Son of Man will send his angels, and they will collect out of his kingdom all causes of sin and all evildoers, 42 and they will throw them into the furnace of fire, where there will be weeping and gnashing of teeth. 43 Then the righteous

Teaching: The Parables

will shine like the sun in the kingdom of their Father. Let anyone with ears listen!"

Three Parables

44 "The kingdom of heaven is like treasure hidden in a field, which someone found and hid; then in his joy he goes and sells all that he has and buys that field."

45 "Again, the kingdom of heaven is like a merchant in **search** of fine pearls; 46 on finding one pearl of great value, he went and sold all that he had and bought it."

47 "Again, the kingdom of heaven is like a net that was thrown into the sea and caught fish of every kind; 48 when it was full, they drew it ashore, sat down, and put the good into baskets but threw out the bad. 49 So it will be at the end of the age. The angels will come out and separate the evil from the righteous 50 and throw them into the furnace of fire, where there will be weeping and gnashing of teeth."

The Parable of the Good Samaritan

Luke 10:25 (NASB) And a lawyer stood up and put Him to the test, saying, "Teacher, what shall I do to inherit eternal life?" 26 And He said to him, "What is written in **the Law**? How does it read to you?" 27 And he answered, "you shall love the Lord your God with all your heart, and with all your soul, and with all your strength, and with all your mind; and your neighbor as yourself." 28 And He said to him, "You have answered correctly; do this and you will live." 29 But wishing to justify himself, he

> *May what I value the most be truly the most valuable.*

> *The word "Law" often stands for the ten commandments.*

said to Jesus, "And **who is my neighbor**?"

30 Jesus replied and said, "A man was going down from Jerusalem to Jericho, and fell among robbers, and they stripped him and beat him, and went away leaving him half dead. 31 And by chance a **priest** was going down on that road, and when he saw him, he passed by on the other side. 32 Likewise a **Levite** also, when he came to the place and saw him, passed by on the other side. 33 But a **Samaritan**, who was on a journey, came upon him; and when he saw him, he felt compassion, 34 and came to him and bandaged up his wounds, pouring oil and wine on them; and he put him on his own beast, and brought him to an inn and took care of him. 35 On the next day he took out two denarii and gave them to the innkeeper and said, 'Take care of him; and whatever more you spend, when I return I will repay you.' 36 Which of these three do you think proved to be a neighbor to the man who fell into the robbers' hands?" 37 And he said, "The one who showed mercy toward him." Then Jesus said to him, "Go and do the same."

The Parable of the Rich Fool

Luke 12:16 (NASB) And He told them a parable, saying, "The land of a rich man was very productive. 17 And he began reasoning to himself, saying, 'What shall I do, since I have no place to store my crops?' 18 Then he said, 'This is what I will do: I will tear down my barns and build larger ones, and there I will store all my grain and my goods. 19 And I will say to my soul, "Soul, you have many

---

Good question.

A priest would be declared "unclean" if he touched blood.

A Levite was a religious official.

Samaritans were looked down upon by the average Jewish person in those days.

Teaching: The Parables

Where am I storing up treasures?

goods laid up for many years to come; take your ease, eat, drink and be merry."' 20 But God said to him, 'You fool! This very night your soul is required of you; and now who will own what you have prepared?' 21 So is the man who stores up **treasure for himself**, and is not rich toward God."

The Parable of the Fig Tree

Luke 13:6 (NASB) And He began telling this parable: "A man had a fig tree which had been planted in his vineyard; and he came looking for fruit on it and did not find any. 7 And he said to the vineyard-keeper, 'Behold, for three years I have come looking for fruit on this fig tree without finding any. Cut it down! Why does it even use up the ground?' 8 And he answered and said to him, 'Let it alone, sir, for

A metaphor for God's patience ... with me.

this year too, until I dig around it and **put in fertilizer**; 9 and if it bears fruit next year, fine; but if not, cut it down.'"

The Parable of the Great Banquet

Luke 14:15 (NASB) When one of those who were reclining at the table with Him heard this, he said to Him, "Blessed is everyone who will eat bread in the kingdom of God!"

The Parable of the Dinner

16 But He said to him, "A man was giving a big dinner, and he invited many; 17 and at the dinner hour he sent his slave to say to those who had been invited, 'Come; for everything is ready now.' 18 But they all alike began to

In other words... I am

make **excuses**. The first one said to him, 'I have bought a piece of land and I need to go out and look at it; please consider me excused.' 19 Another one said, 'I have bought five yoke of oxen, and I am going to try them out; please consider me excused.' 20 Another one said, 'I have married a wife, and for that reason I cannot come.' 21 And the slave came back and reported this to his master. Then the head of the household became angry and said to his slave, 'Go out at once into the streets and lanes of the city and bring in here the poor and crippled and blind and lame.' 22 And the slave said, 'Master, what you commanded has been done, and still there is room.' 23 And the master said to the slave, 'Go out into the highways and along the hedges, and compel them to come in, so that my house may be filled. 24 For I tell you, none of those men who were invited shall taste of my dinner.'"

The Lost Sheep

Luke 15:1 (NASB) Now all the tax collectors and the sinners were coming near Him to listen to Him. 2 Both the Pharisees and the scribes began to grumble, saying, "This man receives sinners and eats with them."

3 So He told them this parable, saying, 4 "What man among you, if he has a hundred sheep and has lost one of them, does not leave the ninety-nine in the open pasture and go after the one which is lost until he finds it? 5 When he has found it, he lays it on his shoulders, rejoicing. 6 And when he comes home, he calls together his friends and his neighbors, saying to them, 'Rejoice with me, for I have found my sheep which was lost!' 7 I tell you that in the same way, there will be more joy

too busy for God and His Kingdom. May I be done with my excuses.

Teaching: The Parables

in heaven over one sinner who repents than over ninety-nine righteous persons who need no repentance."

The Lost Coin

8 "Or what woman, if she has ten silver coins and loses one coin, does not light a lamp and sweep the house and search carefully until she finds it? 9 When she has found it, she calls together her friends and neighbors, saying, 'Rejoice with me, for I have found the coin which I had lost!' 10 In the same way, I tell you, there is joy in the presence of the angels of God over one sinner who repents."

The Prodigal Son

11 And He said, "A man had two sons. 12 The younger of them said to his father, 'Father, give me the share of the estate that falls to me.' So he divided his wealth between them. 13 And not many days later, the younger son gathered everything together and went on a journey into a distant country, and there he squandered his estate with loose living. 14 Now when he had spent everything, a severe famine occurred in that country, and he began to be impoverished. 15 So he went and hired himself out to one of the citizens of that country, and he sent him into his fields to feed **swine**. 16 And he would have gladly filled his stomach with the pods that the swine were eating, and no one was giving anything to him. 17 **But when he came to his senses**, he said, 'How many of my father's hired men have more than enough bread, but I am dying here with hunger! 18 I will get up and go to my fa-

---

Swine (pigs) were unclean animals for Jews.

Was his motive sorrow or hunger?

ther, and will say to him, "Father, I have sinned against heaven, and in your sight; 19 I am no longer worthy to be called your son; make me as one of your hired men."' 20 So he got up and came to his father. **But while he was still a long way off, his father saw him and felt compassion for him, and ran and embraced him and kissed him.** 21 And the son said to him, 'Father, I have sinned against heaven and in your sight; *I am no longer worthy to be called your son.*' 22 But the father said to his slaves, 'Quickly bring out the best robe and put it on him, and put a ring on his hand and sandals on his feet; 23 and bring the fattened calf, kill it, and let us eat and celebrate; 24 for this son of mine was dead and has come to life again; he was lost and has been found.' And they began to celebrate."

25 "Now his older son was in the field, and when he came and approached the house, he heard music and dancing. 26 And he summoned one of the servants and began inquiring what these things could be. 27 And he said to him, 'Your brother has come, and your father has killed the fattened calf because he has received him back safe and sound.' 28 But he became angry and was not willing to go in; and his father came out and began pleading with him. 29 But he answered and said to his father, 'Look! For so many years I have been serving you and I have never neglected a command of yours; and yet you have never given me a young goat, so that I might celebrate with my friends; 30 but when this son of yours came, who has devoured your wealth with prostitutes, you killed the fattened calf

> His father accepted him back before the son even said he was sorry.
>
> The son didn't say, "Make me one of your hired servants," because he had already been accepted back as a son.

Teaching: The Parables

In other words: "I love you as much as your younger brother."

The father loved both sons the same. The elder son could not see his Father's love because he thought he had it coming to him. The younger son finally did see his father's love only when he realized he didn't deserve it.

for him.' 31 And he said to him, '**Son, you have always been with me, and all that is mine is yours**. 32 But we had to celebrate and rejoice, for this brother of yours was dead and has begun to live, and was lost and has been found.'"

Story of the Rich Man and Lazarus

Luke 16:19 (NASB) "Now there was a rich man, and he habitually dressed in purple and fine linen, joyously living in splendor every day. 20 And a poor man named Lazarus was laid at his gate, covered with sores, 21 and longing to be fed with the crumbs which were falling from the rich man's table; besides, even the dogs were coming and licking his sores. 22 Now the poor man died and was carried away by the angels to Abraham's bosom; and the rich man also died and was buried. 23 In Hades he lifted up his eyes, being in torment, and saw Abraham far away and Lazarus in his bosom. 24 And he cried out and said, 'Father Abraham, have mercy on me, and send Lazarus so that he may dip the tip of his finger in water and cool off my tongue, for I am in agony in this flame.' 25 But Abraham said, 'Child, remember that during your life you received your good things, and likewise Lazarus bad things; but now he is being comforted here, and you are in agony. 26 And besides all this, between us and you there is a great chasm fixed, so that those who wish to come over from here to you will not be able, and that none may cross over from there to us.' 27 And he said, 'Then I beg you, father, that you send him to my father's house— 28 for I have five brothers—in order that he may warn them, so that they will not also come to this place of torment.' 29 But Abraham said, 'They have Moses and the Prophets; let them hear them.' 30 But he said, 'No, father Abraham, but if someone goes to them from the dead, they will repent!' 31 But he said to him, '**If they do not listen to Moses and the Prophets, they will not be persuaded even if someone rises from the dead.**'"

> Could I be this deaf and blind to God's Word?

Parable of the Pharisee and the Tax Collector

Luke 18:9 (NASB) And He also told this parable to some people who trusted in themselves that they were righteous, and viewed others with contempt: 10 "Two men went up into the temple to pray, one a Pharisee and the other a tax collector. 11 The Pharisee stood and was praying this to himself: 'God, I thank You that I am not like other people: swindlers, unjust, adulterers, or even like this tax collector. 12 I fast twice a week; I pay tithes of all that I get.' 13 But the tax collector, standing some distance away, was even unwilling to lift up his eyes to heaven, but was beating his breast, saying, 'God, be merciful to me, the sinner!' 14 I tell you, this man went to his house justified rather than the other; for everyone who exalts himself will be humbled, but he who humbles himself will be exalted."

> "I thank God I am humble like the tax collector— not like this Pharisee."

> Uh-oh, I just out-Phariseed the Pharisee.

The Parable of the Ten Bridesmaids

Matthew 25:1 (NRSV) "Then the kingdom of heaven will be like this. Ten bridesmaids took their lamps and went to meet the bridegroom. 2 Five of them were foolish, and five were wise. 3 When the foolish took their lamps, they took

Teaching: The Parables

no oil with them; 4 but the wise took flasks of oil with their lamps. 5 As the bridegroom was delayed, all of them became drowsy and slept. 6 But at midnight there was a shout, 'Look! Here is the bridegroom! Come out to meet him.' 7 Then all those bridesmaids got up and trimmed their lamps. 8 The foolish said to the wise, 'Give us some of your oil, for our lamps are going out.' 9 But the wise replied, 'No! There will not be enough for you and for us; you had better go to the dealers and buy some for yourselves.' 10 And while they went to buy it, the bridegroom came, and those who were ready went with him into the wedding banquet; and the door was shut. 11 Later the other bridesmaids came also, saying, 'Lord, Lord, open to us.' 12 But he replied, 'Truly I tell you, I do not know you.' 13 Keep awake therefore, for you know neither the day nor the hour."

The Parable of the Talents

14 "For it is as if a man, going on a journey, summoned his slaves and entrusted his property to them; 15 to one he gave five talents, to another two, to another one, to each according to his ability. Then he went away. 16 The one who had received the five talents went off at once and traded with them, and made five more talents. 17 In the same way, the one who had the two talents made two more talents. 18 But the one who had received the one talent went off and dug a hole in the ground and hid his master's money. 19 After a long time the master of those slaves came and settled accounts with them. 20 Then the one who had received the five talents came forward, bringing

five more talents, saying, 'Master, you handed over to me five talents; see, I have made five more talents.' 21 His master said to him, 'Well done, good and trustworthy slave; you have been trustworthy in a few things, I will put you in charge of many things; enter into the joy of your master.' 22 And the one with the two talents also came forward, saying, 'Master, you handed over to me two talents; see, I have made two more talents.' 23 His master said to him, 'Well done, good and trustworthy slave; you have been trustworthy in a few things, I will put you in charge of many things; enter into the joy of your master.' 24 Then the one who had received the one talent also came forward, saying, 'Master, I knew that you were a harsh man, reaping where you did not sow, and gathering where you did not scatter seed; 25 so I was afraid, and I went and **hid your talent** in the ground. Here you have what is yours.' 26 But his master replied, 'You wicked and lazy slave! You knew, did you, that I reap where I did not sow, and gather where I did not scatter? 27 Then you ought to have invested my money with the bankers, and on my return I would have received what was my own with interest. 28 So take the talent from him, and give it to the one with the ten talents. 29 For to all those who have, more will be given, and they will have an abundance; but from those who have nothing, even what they have will be taken away. 30 As for this worthless slave, throw him into the outer darkness, where there will be weeping and gnashing of teeth.'"

What am I doing with what I have been given?

How am I hiding the talents I've been given?

The Judgment of the Nations

31 "When the Son of Man comes in his glory, and all the angels with him, then he will sit on the throne of his glory. 32 All the nations will be gathered before him, and he will separate people one from another as a shepherd separates the sheep from the goats, 33 and he will put the sheep at his right hand and the goats at the left. 34 Then the king will say to those at his right hand, 'Come, you that are blessed by my Father, inherit the kingdom prepared for you from the foundation of the world; 35 for I was hungry and you gave me food, I was thirsty and you gave me something to drink, I was a stranger and you welcomed me, 36 I was naked and you gave me clothing, I was sick and you took care of me, I was in prison and you visited me.' 37 Then the righteous will answer him, 'Lord, when was it that we saw you hungry and gave you food, or thirsty and gave you something to drink? 38 And when was it that we saw you a stranger and welcomed you, or naked and gave you clothing? 39 And when was it that we saw you sick or in prison and visited you?' 40 And the king will answer them, 'Truly I tell you, just as you did it to one of the least of these who are members of my family, you did it to me.' 41 Then he will say to those at his left hand, 'You that are accursed, depart from me into the eternal fire prepared for the devil and his angels; 42 for I was hungry and you gave me no food, I was thirsty and you gave me nothing to drink, 43 I was a stranger and you did not welcome me, naked and you did not give me clothing, sick and in prison and you did not visit me.' 44

Then they also will answer, 'Lord, when was it that we saw you hungry or thirsty or a stranger or naked or sick or in prison, and did not take care of you?' 45 Then he will answer them, 'Truly I tell you, just as you did not do it to one of the least of these, you did not do it to me.' 46 And these will go away into eternal punishment, but the righteous into eternal life."

3. The Miracles of Jesus

Water to Wine

John 2:1 (NIV) On the third day a wedding took place at Cana in Galilee. Jesus' mother was there, 2 and Jesus and his disciples had also been invited to the wedding. 3 When the wine was gone, Jesus' mother said to him, "They have no more wine."

4 "Woman, why do you involve me?" Jesus replied. "My hour has not yet come."

5 His mother said to the servants, "Do whatever he tells you."

6 Nearby stood six stone water jars, the kind used by the Jews for ceremonial washing, each holding from twenty to thirty gallons.

7 Jesus said to the servants, "Fill the jars with water"; so they filled them to the brim.

8 Then he told them, "Now draw some out and take it to the master of the banquet."

They did so, 9 and the master of the banquet tasted the water that had been turned into wine. He did not realize where it had come from, though the servants who had drawn the water knew. Then he called the bridegroom aside 10 and said, "Everyone brings out the choice wine first and then the cheaper wine after the guests have had too much to drink; but you have saved the best till now."

11 What Jesus did here in Cana of Galilee was the first of the signs through which he revealed his glory; and his disciples believed in him.

Jesus Heals the Leper

Mark 1:40 (NLT) A man with leprosy came and knelt in front of Jesus, begging to be healed. "If you are willing, you can heal me and make me clean," he said.

41 Moved with compassion, Jesus reached out and **touched him**. "I am willing," he said. "Be healed!" 42 Instantly the leprosy disappeared, and the man was healed.

The Healing at the Pool

John 5:2 (NIV) Now there is in Jerusalem near the Sheep Gate a pool, which in Aramaic is called Bethesda and which is surrounded by five covered colonnades. 3 Here a great number of disabled people used to lie—the blind, the lame, the paralyzed. 5 One who was there had been an invalid for thirty-eight years. 6 When Jesus saw him lying there and learned that he had been in this condition for a long time, he asked him, "Do you want to get well?"

7 "Sir," the invalid replied, "I have no one to help me into the pool when the water is stirred. While I am trying to get in, someone else goes down ahead of me."

8 Then Jesus said to him, "Get up! Pick up your mat and walk." 9 At once the man was cured; he picked up his mat and walked.

The day on which this took place was a Sabbath, 10 and so the Jewish leaders said to the man who had been healed, "It is the Sabbath; the law forbids you to carry your mat."

11 But he replied, "The man who made me well said to me, 'Pick up your mat and walk.' "

Jesus touched the man, a leper, an untouchable, before He healed him as if to say, "I love you, I accept you as you are."

12 So they asked him, "Who is this fellow who told you to pick it up and walk?"

13 The man who was healed had no idea who it was, for Jesus had slipped away into the crowd that was there.

Jesus Heals a Centurion's Servant

Luke 7:1 (NASB) ... He went to Capernaum.

2 And a centurion's slave, who was highly regarded by him, was sick and about to die. 3 When he heard about Jesus, he sent some Jewish elders asking Him to come and save the life of his slave. 4 When they came to Jesus, they earnestly implored Him, saying, "He is worthy for You to grant this to him; 5 for he loves our nation and it was he who built us our synagogue." 6 Now Jesus started on His way with them; and when He was not far from the house, the centurion sent friends, saying to Him, "Lord, do not trouble Yourself further, for I am not worthy for You to come under my roof; 7 for this reason I did not even consider myself worthy to come to You, but just say the word, and my servant will be healed. 8 For I also am a man placed under authority, with soldiers under me; and I say to this one, 'Go!' and he goes, and to another, 'Come!' and he comes, and to my slave, 'Do this!' and he does it." 9 Now when Jesus heard this, He marveled at him, and turned and said to the crowd that was following Him, "I say to you, not even in Israel have I found such great faith." 10 When those who had been sent returned to the house, they found the slave in good health.

The Pigs

Matthew 8:28 (NRSV) When he came to ... the country of the Gadarenes, two demoniacs coming out of the tombs met him. They were so fierce that no one could pass that way. 29 Suddenly they shouted, "What have you to do with us, Son of God? Have you come here to torment us before the time?" 30 Now a large herd of swine was feeding at some distance from them. 31 The demons begged him, "If you cast us out, send us into the herd of swine." 32 And he said to them, "Go!" So they came out and entered the swine; and suddenly, **the whole herd rushed down the steep bank into the sea and perished** in the water. 33 The swineherds ran off, and on going into the town, they told the whole story about what had happened to the demoniacs. 34 Then the whole town came out to meet Jesus; and when they saw him, they begged him to leave their neighborhood.

Jesus Heals in Response to Faith

Mark 5:21 (NLT) Jesus got into the boat again and went back to the other side of the lake, where a large crowd gathered around him on the shore. 22 Then a leader of the local synagogue, whose name was Jairus, arrived. When he saw Jesus, he fell at his feet, 23 pleading fervently with him. "My little daughter is dying," he said. "Please come and lay your hands on her; heal her so she can live."

24 Jesus went with him, and all the people followed, crowding around him. 25 A woman in the crowd had suffered for twelve years with constant bleeding. 26 She had suffered

> I have to realize that the goal of all evil in my life is to destroy me and all I love.

a great deal from many doctors, and over the years she had spent everything she had to pay them, but she had gotten no better. In fact, she had gotten worse. 27 She had heard about Jesus, so she came up behind him through the crowd and touched his robe. 28 For she thought to herself, "If I can just touch his robe, I will be healed." 29 Immediately the bleeding stopped, and she could feel in her body that she had been healed of her terrible condition.

30 Jesus realized at once that healing power had gone out from him, so he turned around in the crowd and asked, "Who touched my robe?"

31 His disciples said to him, "Look at this crowd pressing around you. How can you ask, 'Who touched me?'"

32 But he kept on looking around to see who had done it. 33 Then the frightened woman, trembling at the realization of what had happened to her, came and fell to her knees in front of him and told him what she had done. 34 And he said to her, "Daughter, your faith has made you well. Go in peace. Your suffering is over."

35 While he was still speaking to her, messengers arrived from the home of Jairus, the leader of the synagogue. They told him, "Your daughter is dead. There's no use troubling the Teacher now." 36 But Jesus overheard them and said to Jairus, "Don't be afraid. Just have faith."

37 Then Jesus stopped the crowd and wouldn't let anyone go with him except Peter, James, and John (the brother of James).

38 When they came to the home of the synagogue leader, Jesus saw much commotion and weeping and wailing. 39 He went inside and asked, "Why all this commotion and weeping? The child isn't dead; she's only asleep."

40 The crowd laughed at him. But he made them all leave, and he took the girl's father and mother and his three disciples into the room where the girl was lying. 41 Holding her hand, he said to her, "Talitha koum," which means "Little girl, get up!" 42 And the girl, who was twelve years old, immediately stood up and walked around! They were overwhelmed and totally amazed. 43 Jesus gave them strict orders not to tell anyone what had happened, and then he told them to give her something to eat.

Feeding of the 5,000

{Jesus withdrew to Bethsaida but the crowds followed Him.}

Luke 9:11 (NASB) He began speaking to them about the kingdom of God and curing those who had need of healing.

12 Now the day was ending, and the twelve came and said to Him, "Send the crowd away, that they may go into the surrounding villages and countryside and find lodging and get something to eat; for here we are in a desolate place." 13 But He said to them, "You give them something to eat!" And they said, "We have no more than five loaves and two fish, unless perhaps we go and buy food for all these people." 14 (For there were about five thousand men.) And He said to His disciples, "Have them sit

The people in Jesus' day would have remembered that Elisha the prophet, who lived hundreds of years before, did this same miracle — multiplying loaves of bread to

The Miracles of Jesus

feed 100 men in this same region of Israel.
2 Kings 4, pg 112.

down to eat in groups of about fifty each." 15 They did so, and had them all sit down. 16 Then He took the five loaves and the two fish, and looking up to heaven, He blessed them, and broke them, and kept giving them to the disciples to set before the people. 17 And they all ate and were satisfied; and the broken pieces which they had left over were picked up, twelve baskets full.

Jesus Walks on the Water

Matthew 14:22 (NRSV) ... he made the disciples get into the boat and go on ahead to the other side, while he dismissed the crowds. 23 And after he had dismissed the crowds, he went up the mountain by himself to pray. When evening came, he was there alone, but by this time the boat, battered by the waves, was far from the land, for the wind was against them. 25 And early in the morning he came walking toward them on the sea. 26 But when the disciples saw him walking on the sea, they were terrified, saying, "It is a ghost!" And they cried out in fear. 27 But immediately Jesus spoke to them and said, "Take heart, it is I; do not be afraid."

Prayer 1: Lord keep my eyes on Jesus, not the storm.

28 Peter answered him, "Lord, if it is you, command me to come to you on the water." 29 He said, "Come." So Peter got out of the boat, started walking on the water, and came toward Jesus. 30 But when he noticed the strong wind, he became frightened, and **beginning to sink**, he cried out, "Lord, save me!" 31 Jesus immediately reached out his hand and caught him, saying to him, "You of little faith, why did you doubt?" 32 When they got

into the boat, the wind ceased. 33 And those in the boat worshiped him, saying, "Truly you are the Son of God."

Blind Man at Bethsaida

Mark 8:22 (NLT) When they arrived at Bethsaida, some people brought a blind man to Jesus, and they begged him to touch the man and heal him. 23 Jesus took the blind man by the hand and led him out of the village. Then, spitting on the man's eyes, he laid his hands on him and asked, "Can you see anything now?"

24 The man looked around. "Yes," he said, "I see people, but I can't see them very clearly. They look like trees walking around."

25 Then Jesus placed his hands on the man's eyes again, and his eyes were opened. His sight was completely restored, and he could see everything clearly.

Boy with Evil Spirit

Mark 9:17 (NLT) One of the men in the crowd spoke up and said, "Teacher, I brought my son so you could heal him. He is possessed by an evil spirit that won't let him talk. 18 And whenever this spirit seizes him, it throws him violently to the ground. Then he foams at the mouth and grinds his teeth and becomes rigid. So I asked your disciples to cast out the evil spirit, but they couldn't do it."

19 Jesus said to them, "You faithless people! How long must I be with you? How long must I put up with you? Bring the boy to me."

20 So they brought the boy. But when the evil spirit saw Jesus, it threw the child into a

Prayer 2: Lord help me stay in the boat.

The Miracles of Jesus

violent convulsion, and he fell to the ground, writhing and foaming at the mouth.

21 "How long has this been happening?" Jesus asked the boy's father.

He replied, "Since he was a little boy. 22 The spirit often throws him into the fire or into water, trying to kill him. Have mercy on us and help us, if you can."

23 "What do you mean, 'If I can?'" Jesus asked. "Anything is possible if a person believes."

24 The father instantly cried out, "*I do believe, but help me overcome my unbelief!*"

25 When Jesus saw that the crowd of onlookers was growing, he rebuked the evil spirit. "Listen, you spirit that makes this boy unable to hear and speak," he said. "I command you to come out of this child and never enter him again!"

26 Then the spirit screamed and threw the boy into another violent convulsion and left him. The boy appeared to be dead. A murmur ran through the crowd as people said, "He's dead." 27 But Jesus took him by the hand and helped him to his feet, and he stood up.

28 Afterward, when Jesus was alone in the house with his disciples, they asked him, "Why couldn't we cast out that evil spirit?"

29 Jesus replied, "This kind can be cast out only by prayer."

Could doubt sometimes be the evidence of faith? Don't I have to first believe something before I can doubt it?

4. The Plot to Kill Jesus

{Jesus raised his friend Lazarus from the dead. The common people were thrilled; the religious leaders were fearful.}

The Plot to Kill Jesus

John 11:45 (NIV) Therefore many of the Jews who had come to visit Mary, and had seen what Jesus did, believed in him. 46 But some of them went to the Pharisees and told them what Jesus had done. 47 Then the chief priests and the Pharisees called a meeting of the Sanhedrin.

"What are we accomplishing?" they asked. "Here is this man performing many signs. 48 If we let him go on like this, everyone will believe in him, and then the Romans will come and take away both our temple and our nation."

49 Then one of them, named Caiaphas, who was high priest that year, spoke up, "You know nothing at all! 50 You do not realize that it is better for you that one man die for the people than that the whole nation perish."

51 He did not say this on his own, but as high priest that year he prophesied that Jesus would die for the Jewish nation, 52 and not only for that nation but also for the scattered children of God, to bring them together and make them one. 53 So from that day on they plotted to take his life.

54 Therefore Jesus no longer moved about publicly among the people of Judea. Instead he withdrew to a region near the wilderness, to a village called Ephraim, where he stayed

The Plot to Kill Jesus 74

(margin note: Exodus 12, pg. 107.)

with his disciples.

55 When it was almost time for the Jewish **Passover**, many went up from the country to Jerusalem for their ceremonial cleansing before the Passover. 56 They kept looking for Jesus, and as they stood in the temple courts they asked one another, "What do you think? Isn't he coming to the festival at all?" 57 But the chief priests and the Pharisees had given orders that anyone who found out where Jesus was should report it so that they might arrest him.

Jesus Anointed at Bethany

John 12:1 (NIV) Six days before the Passover, Jesus came to Bethany, where Lazarus lived, whom Jesus had raised from the dead. 2 Here a dinner was given in Jesus' honor. Martha served, while Lazarus was among those reclining at the table with him. 3 Then Mary took about a pint of pure nard, an expensive perfume; she poured it on Jesus' feet and wiped his feet with her hair. And the house was filled with the fragrance of the perfume.

4 But one of his disciples, Judas Iscariot, who was later to betray him, objected, 5 "Why wasn't this perfume sold and the money given to the poor? It was worth a year's wages." 6 He did not say this because he cared about the poor but because he was a thief; as keeper of the money bag, he used to help himself to what was put into it.

7 "Leave her alone," Jesus replied. "It was intended that she should save this perfume for the day of my burial. 8 You will always have

the poor among you, but you will not always have me."

9 Meanwhile a large crowd of Jews found out that Jesus was there and came, not only because of him but also to see Lazarus, whom he had raised from the dead. 10 So the chief priests made plans to kill Lazarus as well, 11 for on account of him many of the Jews were going over to Jesus and believing in him.

Jesus Comes to Jerusalem as King

12 The next day the great crowd that had come for the festival heard that Jesus was on his way to Jerusalem. 13 They took palm branches and went out to meet him, shouting,

"Hosanna!"

"Blessed is he who comes in the name of the Lord!"

"Blessed is the king of Israel!"

14 Jesus found a young donkey and sat on it, as it is written:

15 **"Do not be afraid, Daughter Zion; see, your king is coming, seated on a donkey's colt."**

Zechariah 9:9, pg. 135.

Luke 19:39 (NASB) Some of the Pharisees in the crowd said to Him, "Teacher, rebuke Your disciples." 40 But Jesus answered, "I tell you, if these become silent, the stones will cry out!"

41 When He approached Jerusalem, He saw the city and wept over it, 42 saying, "If you had known in this day, even you, the things which make for peace! But now they have been hidden from your eyes. 43 For the days will come upon you when your enemies will throw up a

The Plot to Kill Jesus

barricade against you, and surround you and hem you in on every side, 44 and they will level you to the ground and your children within you, and they will not leave in you one stone upon another, because you did not recognize the time of your visitation."

Traders Driven from the Temple

45 Jesus entered the temple and began to drive out those who were selling, 46 saying to them, "It is written, 'and my house shall be a house of prayer,' but you have made it a robbers' den."

47 And He was teaching daily in the temple; but the chief priests and the scribes and the leading men among the people were trying to destroy Him, 48 and they could not find anything that they might do, for all the people were hanging on to every word He said.

Jesus Anointed at Bethany

Mark 14:1 (NLT) It was now two days before Passover and the Festival of Unleavened Bread. The leading priests and the teachers of religious law were still looking for an opportunity to capture Jesus secretly and kill him. 2 "But not during the Passover celebration," they agreed, "or the people may riot."

Judas Agrees to Betray Jesus

10 Then Judas Iscariot, one of the twelve disciples, went to the leading priests to arrange to betray Jesus to them. 11 They were delighted when they heard why he had come, and they promised to give him money. So he began looking for an opportunity to betray Jesus.

The Last Supper

12 On the first day of the Festival of Unleavened Bread, when the Passover lamb is sacrificed, Jesus' disciples asked him, "Where do you want us to go to prepare the Passover meal for you?"

13 So Jesus sent two of them into Jerusalem with these instructions: "As you go into the city, a man carrying a pitcher of water will meet you. Follow him. 14 At the house he enters, say to the owner, 'The Teacher asks: Where is the guest room where I can eat the Passover meal with my disciples?' 15 He will take you upstairs to a large room that is already set up. That is where you should prepare our meal." 16 So the two disciples went into the city and found everything just as Jesus had said, and they prepared the Passover meal there.

17 In the evening Jesus arrived with the twelve disciples.

Jesus Washes His Disciples' Feet

John 13:1 (NIV) It was just before the Passover Festival. Jesus knew that the hour had come for him to leave this world and go to the Father. Having loved his own who were in the world, he loved them to the end.

2 The evening meal was in progress, and the devil had already prompted Judas, the son of Simon Iscariot, to betray Jesus. 3 Jesus knew that the Father had put all things under his power, and that he had come from God and was returning to God; 4 so he got up from the meal, took off his outer clothing, and wrapped a towel around his waist. 5 After that, he

poured water into a basin and began to wash his disciples' feet, drying them with the towel that was wrapped around him.

6 He came to Simon Peter, who said to him, "Lord, are you going to wash my feet?"

7 Jesus replied, "You do not realize now what I am doing, but later you will understand."

8 "No," said Peter, "you shall never wash my feet."

Jesus answered, "Unless I wash you, you have no part with me."

9 "Then, Lord," Simon Peter replied, "not just my feet but my hands and my head as well!"

10 Jesus answered, "Those who have had a bath need only to wash their feet; their whole body is clean. And you are clean, though not every one of you." 11 For he knew who was going to betray him, and that was why he said not every one was clean.

12 When he had finished washing their feet, he put on his clothes and returned to his place. "Do you understand what I have done for you?" he asked them. 13 "You call me 'Teacher' and 'Lord,' and rightly so, for that is what I am. 14 Now that I, your Lord and Teacher, have washed your feet, you also should wash one another's feet. 15 I have set you an example that you should do as I have done for you. 16 Very truly I tell you, no servant is greater than his master, nor is a messenger greater than the one who sent him. 17 Now that you know these things, you will be blessed if you do them.

Mark 14:18 (NLT) As they were at the table eating, Jesus said, "I tell you the truth, one of you eating with me here will betray me."

19 Greatly distressed, each one asked in turn, "Am I the one?"

20 He replied, "It is one of you twelve who is eating from this bowl with me. 21 For the Son of Man must die, as the Scriptures declared long ago. But how terrible it will be for the one who betrays him. It would be far better for that man if he had never been born!"

22 As they were eating, Jesus took some bread and blessed it. Then he broke it in pieces and gave it to the disciples, saying, "Take it, for this is my body."

23 And he took a cup of wine and gave thanks to God for it. He gave it to them, and they all drank from it. 24 And he said to them, "This is my blood, which confirms the covenant between God and his people. It is poured out as a sacrifice for many. 25 I tell you the truth, I will not drink wine again until the day I drink it new in the Kingdom of God."

Your Sorrow Will Turn into Joy

John 16:16 (NIV) Jesus went on to say, "In a little while you will see me no more, and then after a little while you will see me."

17 At this, some of his disciples said to one another, "What does he mean by saying, 'In a little while you will see me no more, and then after a little while you will see me,' and 'Because I am going to the Father'?" 18 They kept asking, "What does he mean by 'a little while'? We don't understand what he is saying."

The Plot to Kill Jesus

Habakkuk 3:17, pg. 133.

19 Jesus saw that they wanted to ask him about this, so he said to them, "Are you asking one another what I meant when I said, 'In a little while you will see me no more, and then after a little while you will see me'? 20 Very truly I tell you, you will weep and mourn while the world rejoices. **You will grieve, but your grief will turn to joy.** 21 A woman giving birth to a child has pain because her time has come; but when her baby is born she forgets the anguish because of her joy that a child is born into the world. 22 So with you: Now is your time of grief, but I will see you again and you will rejoice, and no one will take away your joy.

Mark 14:26 (NLT) Then they sang a hymn and went out to the Mount of Olives.

Jesus Predicts Peter's Denial

27 On the way, Jesus told them, "All of you will desert me. For the Scriptures say,

'God will strike the Shepherd, and the sheep will be scattered.'

28 But after I am raised from the dead, I will go ahead of you to Galilee and meet you there."

29 Peter said to him, "Even if everyone else deserts you, I never will."

30 Jesus replied, "I tell you the truth, Peter—this very night, before the rooster crows twice, you will deny three times that you even know me."

31 "No!" Peter declared emphatically. "Even if I have to die with you, I will never deny you!" And all the others vowed the same.

Jesus Prays in Gethsemane

32 They went to the olive grove called Gethsemane, and Jesus said, "Sit here while I go and pray." 33 He took Peter, James, and John with him, and he became deeply troubled and distressed. 34 He told them, "My soul is crushed with grief to the point of death. Stay here and keep watch with me."

35 He went on a little farther and fell to the ground. He prayed that, if it were possible, the awful hour awaiting him might pass him by. 36 "Abba, Father," he cried out, "everything is possible for you. Please take this cup of suffering away from me. Yet **I want your will to be done, not mine.**"

> I would like the faith to pray this prayer.

37 Then he returned and found the disciples asleep. He said to Peter, "Simon, are you asleep? Couldn't you watch with me even one hour? 38 Keep watch and pray, so that you will not give in to temptation. For the spirit is willing, but the body is weak."

39 Then Jesus left them again and prayed the same prayer as before. 40 When he returned to them again, he found them sleeping, for they couldn't keep their eyes open. And they didn't know what to say.

41 When he returned to them the third time, he said, "Go ahead and sleep. Have your rest. But no—the time has come. The Son of Man is betrayed into the hands of sinners. 42 Up, let's be going. Look, my betrayer is here!"

Jesus Is Betrayed and Arrested

43 And immediately, even as Jesus said this, Judas, one of the twelve disciples, arrived with

The Plot to Kill Jesus

a crowd of men armed with swords and clubs. They had been sent by the leading priests, the teachers of religious law, and the elders. 44 The traitor, Judas, had given them a prearranged signal: "You will know which one to arrest when I greet him with a kiss. Then you can take him away under guard." 45 As soon as they arrived, Judas walked up to Jesus. "Rabbi!" he exclaimed, and gave him the kiss.

46 Then the others grabbed Jesus and arrested him. 47 But one of the men with Jesus pulled out his sword and struck the high priest's slave, slashing off his ear.

48 Jesus asked them, "Am I some dangerous revolutionary, that you come with swords and clubs to arrest me? 49 Why didn't you arrest me in the Temple? I was there among you teaching every day. But these things are happening to fulfill what the Scriptures say about me."

50 Then all his disciples deserted him and ran away. 51 One young man following behind was clothed only in a long linen shirt. When the mob tried to grab him, 52 he slipped out of his shirt and ran away naked.

Jesus Before the Council

53 They took Jesus to the high priest's home where the leading priests, the elders, and the teachers of religious law had gathered. 54 Meanwhile, Peter followed him at a distance and went right into the high priest's courtyard. There he sat with the guards, warming himself by the fire.

55 Inside, the leading priests and the en-

tire high council were trying to find evidence against Jesus, so they could put him to death. But they couldn't find any. 56 Many false witnesses spoke against him, but they contradicted each other. 57 Finally, some men stood up and gave this false testimony: 58 "We heard him say, 'I will destroy this Temple made with human hands, and in three days I will build another, made without human hands.'" 59 But even then they didn't get their stories straight!

60 Then the high priest stood up before the others and asked Jesus, "Well, aren't you going to answer these charges? What do you have to say for yourself?" 61 But **Jesus was silent** and made no reply. Then the high priest asked him, "Are you the Messiah, the Son of the Blessed One?"

62 Jesus said, "I AM. And you will see the Son of Man seated in the place of power at God's right hand and coming on the clouds of heaven."

63 Then the high priest tore his clothing to show his horror and said, "Why do we need other witnesses? 64 You have all heard his blasphemy. What is your verdict?"

"Guilty!" they all cried. "He deserves to die!"

65 Then some of them began to spit at him, and they blindfolded him and beat him with their fists. "Prophesy to us," they jeered. And the guards slapped him as they took him away.

Peter Denies Jesus

66 Meanwhile, Peter was in the courtyard below. One of the servant girls who worked for the high priest came by 67 and noticed Peter

Isaiah 53:7, pg. 120.

The Plot to Kill Jesus

warming himself at the fire. She looked at him closely and said, "You were one of those with Jesus of Nazareth."

68 But Peter denied it. "I don't know what you're talking about," he said, and he went out into the entryway. Just then, a rooster crowed.

69 When the servant girl saw him standing there, she began telling the others, "This man is definitely one of them!" 70 But Peter denied it again.

A little later some of the other bystanders confronted Peter and said, "You must be one of them, because you are a Galilean."

71 Peter swore, "A curse on me if I'm lying—I don't know this man you're talking about!" 72 And immediately the rooster crowed the second time.

Suddenly, Jesus' words flashed through Peter's mind: "Before the rooster crows twice, you will deny three times that you even know me." And he broke down and wept.

Jesus Brought Before Pilate

Matthew 27:1 (NRSV) When morning came, all the chief priests and the elders of the people conferred together against Jesus in order to bring about his death. 2 They bound him, led him away, and handed him over to Pilate the governor.

The Suicide of Judas

3 When Judas, his betrayer, saw that Jesus was condemned, he repented and brought back the thirty pieces of silver to the chief priests and the elders. 4 He said, "I have

sinned by betraying innocent blood." But they said, "What is that to us? See to it yourself." 5 Throwing down the pieces of silver in the temple, he departed; and he went and hanged himself. 6 But the chief priests, taking the pieces of silver, said, "It is not lawful to put them into the treasury, since they are blood money." 7 After conferring together, they used them to buy the potter's field as a place to bury foreigners. 8 For this reason that field has been called the Field of Blood to this day. 9 Then was fulfilled what had been spoken through the prophet Jeremiah, "And they took the **thirty pieces of silver**, the price of the one on whom a price had been set, on whom some of the people of Israel had set a price, 10 and they gave them for the **potter's field**, as the Lord commanded me."

This was predicted by the prophet Zechariah hundreds of years before.

Zechariah 11:12,13; pg 135.

Pilate Questions Jesus

11 Now Jesus stood before the governor; and the governor asked him, "Are you the King of the Jews?" Jesus said, "You say so." 12 But when he was accused by the chief priests and elders, he did not answer. 13 Then Pilate said to him, "Do you not hear how many accusations they make against you?" 14 But he gave him no answer, not even to a single charge, so that the governor was greatly amazed.

Jesus Before Herod

Luke 23:8 (NASB) Now Herod was very glad when he saw Jesus; for he had wanted to see Him for a long time, because he had been hearing about Him and was hoping to see some sign performed by Him. 9 And he ques-

The Plot to Kill Jesus

tioned Him at some length; but He answered him nothing. 10 And the chief priests and the scribes were standing there, accusing Him vehemently. 11 And Herod with his soldiers, after treating Him with contempt and mocking Him, dressed Him in a gorgeous robe and sent Him back to Pilate. 12 Now Herod and Pilate became friends with one another that very day; for before they had been enemies with each other.

Pilate Seeks Jesus' Release

13 Pilate summoned the chief priests and the rulers and the people, 14 and said to them, "You brought this man to me as one who incites the people to rebellion, and behold, having examined Him before you, I have found no guilt in this man regarding the charges which you make against Him. 15 No, nor has Herod, for he sent Him back to us; and behold, nothing deserving death has been done by Him. 16 Therefore I will punish Him and release Him." 17 (Now he was obliged to release to them at the feast one prisoner.)

18 But they cried out all together, saying, "Away with this man, and release for us Barabbas!" 19 (He was one who had been thrown into prison for an insurrection made in the city, and for murder.) 20 Pilate, wanting to release Jesus, addressed them again, 21 but they kept on calling out, saying, "Crucify, crucify Him!" 22 And he said to them the third time, "Why, what evil has this man done? I have found in Him no guilt demanding death; therefore I will punish Him and release Him." 23 But they were insistent, with loud voices asking that He

be crucified. And their voices began to prevail. 24 And Pilate pronounced sentence that their demand be granted. 25 And he released the man they were asking for who had been thrown into prison for insurrection and murder, but he delivered Jesus to their will.

Jesus Sentenced to Be Crucified

John 19:1 (NIV) Then Pilate took Jesus and had him flogged. 2 The soldiers twisted together a crown of thorns and put it on his head. They clothed him in a purple robe 3 and went up to him again and again, saying, "Hail, king of the Jews!" And they slapped him in the face.

4 Once more Pilate came out and said to the Jews gathered there, "Look, I am bringing him out to you to let you know that I find no basis for a charge against him." 5 When Jesus came out wearing the crown of thorns and the purple robe, Pilate said to them, "Here is the man!"

6 As soon as the chief priests and their officials saw him, they shouted, "Crucify! Crucify!"

But Pilate answered, "You take him and crucify him. As for me, I find no basis for a charge against him."

7 The Jewish leaders insisted, "We have a law, and according to that law he must die, because he claimed to be the Son of God."

8 When Pilate heard this, he was even more afraid, 9 and he went back inside the palace. "Where do you come from?" he asked Jesus, but Jesus gave him no answer. 10 "Do you refuse to speak to me?" Pilate said. "Don't you realize I have power either to free you or to crucify you?"

The Plot to Kill Jesus

11 Jesus answered, "You would have no power over me if it were not given to you from above. Therefore the one who handed me over to you is guilty of a greater sin."

12 From then on, Pilate tried to set Jesus free, but the Jewish leaders kept shouting, "If you let this man go, you are no friend of Caesar. Anyone who claims to be a king opposes Caesar."

13 When Pilate heard this, he brought Jesus out and sat down on the judge's seat at a place known as the Stone Pavement (which in Aramaic is Gabbatha). 14 It was the day of Preparation of the Passover; it was about noon.

"Here is your king," Pilate said to the Jews.

15 But they shouted, "Take him away! Take him away! Crucify him!"

"Shall I crucify your king?" Pilate asked.

"We have no king but Caesar," the chief priests answered.

16 Finally Pilate handed him over to them to be crucified.

17 Carrying his own cross, he went out to the place of the Skull (which in Aramaic is called Golgotha).

5. The Death of Jesus

Simon Bears the Cross

Luke 23:26 (NASB) When they led Him away, they seized a man, Simon of Cyrene, coming in from the country, and placed on him the cross to carry behind Jesus.

27 And following Him was a large crowd of the people, and of women who were mourning and lamenting Him. 28 But Jesus turning to them said, "Daughters of Jerusalem, stop weeping for Me, but weep for yourselves and for your children. 29 For behold, the days are coming when they will say, 'Blessed are the barren, and the wombs that never bore, and the breasts that never nursed.' 30 Then they will begin to say to the mountains, 'fall on us,' and to the hills, 'cover us.' 31 For if they do these things when the tree is green, what will happen when it is dry?"

32 Two others also, who were criminals, were being led away to be put to death with Him.

The Crucifixion

33 When they came to the place called The Skull, there they crucified Him and the criminals, one on the right and the other on the left.

The Death of Jesus

The 7 Words of the Cross

Word One ...

Luke 23:34 (NASB) But Jesus was saying, "Father, forgive them; for they do not know what they are doing." 35 And the people stood by, looking on. And even the rulers were sneering at Him, saying, "He saved others; let Him save Himself if this is the Christ of God, His Chosen One."

36 The soldiers also mocked Him, coming up to Him, offering Him sour wine, 37 and saying, "If You are the King of the Jews, save Yourself!" 38 Now there was also an inscription above Him, "this is the king of the Jews."

Word Two ...

Luke 23:39 (NASB) One of the criminals who were hanged there was hurling abuse at Him, saying, "Are You not the Christ? Save Yourself and us!" 40 But the other answered, and rebuking him said, "Do you not even fear God, since you are under the same sentence of condemnation? 41 And we indeed are suffering justly, for we are receiving what we deserve for our deeds; but this man has done nothing wrong." 42 And he was saying, "Jesus, remember me when You come in Your kingdom!" 43 And He said to him, "Truly I say to you, today you shall be with Me in Paradise."

Word Three ...

John 19:23 (NIV) When the soldiers crucified Jesus, they took his clothes, dividing them into four shares, one for each of them, with the undergarment remaining. This garment was seamless, woven in one piece from top to bottom.

24 "Let's not tear it," they said to one another. "Let's decide by lot who will get it."

This happened that the **scripture** might be fulfilled that said,

"They divided my clothes among them and cast lots for my garment."

So this is what the soldiers did.

25 Near the cross of Jesus stood his mother, his mother's sister, Mary the wife of Clopas, and Mary Magdalene. 26 When Jesus saw his mother there, and the disciple whom he loved standing nearby, he said to her, "Woman, here is your son," 27 and to the disciple, "Here is your mother." From that time on, this disciple took her into his home.

Word Four ...

Mark 15:33 (NLT) At noon, darkness fell across the whole land until three o'clock. 34 Then at three o'clock Jesus called out with a loud voice, "Eloi, Eloi, lema sabachthani?" which means *"**My God, my God, why have you abandoned me?**"*

Word Five ...

John 19:28 (NIV) Later, knowing that everything had now been finished, and so that **Scripture would be fulfilled**, Jesus said, "I am thirsty." 29 A jar of **wine** vinegar was there, so they soaked a sponge in it, put the sponge on a stalk of the **hyssop** plant, and **lifted** it to Jesus' lips.

Psalm 22:18; pg. 118.

These words are from Psalm 22:1, pg. 118.

What scripture was fulfilled? Why a stalk of the hyssop plant? Exodus 12, pg 107.

The Death of Jesus

Jesus was not finished, His work on the cross was finished.

Whose hands is my life in?

The curtain separated the Holy part of the temple from the Holy of Holies — the room reserved for God. Jesus is the way to God's presence.

Word Six ...

30 When he had received the drink, Jesus said, "It is **finished**."

Word Seven ...

Luke 23:46 (NASB) And Jesus, crying out with a loud voice, said, "**Father, into your hands I commit my spirit**." Having said this, He breathed His last.

The Story Continues ....

Matthew 27:51 (NRSV) At that moment the **curtain** of the temple was torn in two, from top to bottom. The earth shook, and the rocks were split. 52 The tombs also were opened, and many bodies of the saints who had fallen asleep were raised. 53 After his resurrection they came out of the tombs and entered the holy city and appeared to many. 54 Now when the centurion and those with him, who were keeping watch over Jesus, saw the earthquake and what took place, they were terrified and said, "Truly this man was God's Son!"

55 Many women were also there, looking on from a distance; they had followed Jesus from Galilee and had provided for him. 56 Among them were Mary Magdalene, and Mary the mother of James and Joseph, and the mother of the sons of Zebedee.

The Death of Jesus

John 19:31 (NIV) Now it was the day of Preparation, and the next day was to be a special Sabbath. Because the Jewish leaders did not want the bodies left on the crosses during the Sabbath, they asked Pilate to have the legs broken and the bodies taken down. 32 The soldiers therefore came and broke the legs of the first man who had been crucified with Jesus, and then those of the other. 33 But when they came to Jesus and found that he was already dead, they did not break his legs. 34 Instead, one of the soldiers **pierced** Jesus' side with a spear, bringing a sudden flow of blood and water. 35 The man who saw it has given testimony, and his testimony is true. He knows that he tells the truth, and he testifies so that you also may believe. 36 These things happened so that the scripture would be fulfilled: **"Not one of his bones will be broken,"** 37 and, as another scripture says, "They will look on the one they have pierced."

Isaiah 53:7, pg. 120.

Exodus 12 regulations for the Passover lamb (pg. 107).

The Burial of Jesus

Mark 15:42 (NLT) This all happened on Friday, the day of preparation, the day before the Sabbath. As evening approached, 43 Joseph of Arimathea took a risk and went to Pilate and asked for Jesus' body. (Joseph was an honored member of the high council, and he was waiting for the Kingdom of God to come.) 44 Pilate couldn't believe that Jesus was already dead, so he called for the Roman officer and asked if he had died yet. 45 The officer confirmed that Jesus was dead, so Pilate told Joseph he could have the body.

John 19:38 (NIV) Later, Joseph of Arimathea asked Pilate for the body of Jesus. Now Joseph was a disciple of Jesus, but secretly because he feared the Jewish leaders. With Pi-

The Death of Jesus

[margin: John 3, pg. 18.]

late's permission, he came and took the body away. 39 He was accompanied by Nicodemus, the man who earlier had visited Jesus at night. **Nicodemus** brought a mixture of myrrh and aloes, about seventy-five pounds. 40 Taking Jesus' body, the two of them wrapped it, with the spices, in strips of linen. This was in accordance with Jewish burial customs. 41 At the place where Jesus was crucified, there was a garden, and in the garden a new tomb, in which no one had ever been laid. 42 Because it was the Jewish day of Preparation and since the tomb was nearby, they laid Jesus there.

Luke 23:55 (NASB) Now the women who had come with Him out of Galilee followed, and saw the tomb and how His body was laid. 56 Then they returned and prepared spices and perfumes.

[margin: The Sabbath was a Saturday.]

And on the **Sabbath** they rested according to the commandment.

6. The Resurrection of Jesus

The Guard at the Tomb

Matthew 27:62 (NRSV) The next day, that is, after the day of Preparation, the chief priests and the Pharisees gathered before Pilate 63 and said, "Sir, we remember what that impostor said while he was still alive, 'After three days I will rise again.' 64 Therefore command the tomb to be made secure until the third day; otherwise his disciples may go and steal him away, and tell the people, 'He has been raised from the dead,' and the last deception would be worse than the first." 65 Pilate said to them, "You have a guard of soldiers; go, make it as secure as you can." 66 So they went with the guard and made the tomb secure by sealing the stone.

The Empty Tomb

John 20:1 (NIV) Early on the **first day of the week**, while it was still dark, Mary Magdalene went to the tomb and saw that the stone had been removed from the entrance. 2 So she came running to Simon Peter and the other disciple, the one Jesus loved, and said, "They have taken the Lord out of the tomb, and we don't know where they have put him!"

3 So Peter and the other disciple started for the tomb. 4 Both were running, but the other disciple outran Peter and reached the tomb first. 5 He bent over and looked in at the strips of linen lying there but did not go in. 6 Then Simon Peter came along behind him and went straight into the tomb. He saw the strips of linen lying there, 7 as well as the cloth that

Sunday

The Resurrection of Jesus

had been wrapped around Jesus' head. The cloth was still lying in its place, separate from the linen. 8 Finally the other disciple, who had reached the tomb first, also went inside. He saw and believed. 9 (They still did not understand from Scripture that Jesus had to rise from the dead.) 10 Then the disciples went back to where they were staying.

Jesus Appears to Mary Magdalene

11 Now Mary stood outside the tomb crying. As she wept, she bent over to look into the tomb 12 and saw two angels in white, seated where Jesus' body had been, one at the head and the other at the foot.

13 They asked her, "Woman, why are you crying?"

"They have taken my Lord away," she said, "and I don't know where they have put him." 14 At this, she turned around and saw Jesus standing there, but she did not realize that it was Jesus.

15 He asked her, "Woman, why are you crying? Who is it you are looking for?"

Thinking he was the gardener, she said, "Sir, if you have carried him away, tell me where you have put him, and I will get him."

16 Jesus said to her, "Mary."

She turned toward him and cried out in Aramaic, "Rabboni!" (which means "Teacher").

17 Jesus said, "Do not hold on to me, for I have not yet ascended to the Father. Go instead to my brothers and tell them, 'I am ascending to my Father and your Father, to my

God and your God.'"

18 Mary Magdalene went to the disciples with the news: "I have seen the Lord!" And she told them that he had said these things to her.

The Report of the Guard

Matthew 28:11 (NRSV) While they were going, some of the guard went into the city and told the chief priests everything that had happened. 12 After the priests had assembled with the elders, they devised a plan to give a large sum of money to the soldiers, 13 telling them, "You must say, 'His disciples came by night and stole him away while we were asleep.' 14 If this comes to the governor's ears, we will satisfy him and keep you out of trouble." 15 So they took the money and did as they were directed. And this story is still told among the Jews to this day.

The Road to Emmaus

Luke 24:13 (NASB) And behold, two of them (followers of Jesus) were going that very day to a village named Emmaus, which was about seven miles from Jerusalem. 14 And they were talking with each other about all these things which had taken place. 15 While they were talking and discussing, Jesus Himself approached and began traveling with them. 16 But their eyes were prevented from recognizing Him. 17 And He said to them, "What are these words that you are exchanging with one another as you are walking?" And they stood still, looking sad. 18 One of them, named Cleopas, answered and said to Him, "Are You the only one visiting Jerusalem and

The Resurrection of Jesus

unaware of the things which have happened here in these days?" 19 And He said to them, "What things?" And they said to Him, "The things about Jesus the Nazarene, who was a prophet mighty in deed and word in the sight of God and all the people, 20 and how the chief priests and our rulers delivered Him to the sentence of death, and crucified Him. 21 But we were hoping that it was He who was going to redeem Israel. Indeed, besides all this, it is the third day since these things happened. 22 But also some women among us amazed us. When they were at the tomb early in the morning, 23 and did not find His body, they came, saying that they had also seen a vision of angels who said that He was alive. 24 Some of those who were with us went to the tomb and found it just exactly as the women also had said; but Him they did not see." 25 And He said to them, "O foolish men and slow of heart to believe in all that the prophets have spoken! 26 Was it not necessary for the Christ to suffer these things and to enter into His glory?" 27 Then beginning with **Moses and with all the prophets**, He explained to them the things concerning Himself in all the Scriptures.

This was a short cut way of referring to the entire Old Testament.

28 And they approached the village where they were going, and He acted as though He were going farther. 29 But they urged Him, saying, "Stay with us, for it is getting toward evening, and the day is now nearly over." So He went in to stay with them. 30 When He had reclined at the table with them, He took the bread and blessed it, and breaking it, He began giving it to them. 31 Then their eyes were opened and they recognized Him; and

He vanished from their sight. 32 They said to one another, "Were not our hearts burning within us while He was speaking to us on the road, while He was explaining the Scriptures to us?" 33 And they got up that very hour and returned to Jerusalem, and found gathered together the eleven and those who were with them, 34 saying, "The Lord has really risen and has appeared to Simon." 35 They began to relate their experiences on the road and how He was recognized by them in the breaking of the bread.

Jesus Appears to His Disciples

John 20:19 (NIV) On the evening of that first day of the week, when the disciples were together, with the doors locked for fear of the Jewish leaders, Jesus came and stood among them and said, "Peace be with you!" 20 After he said this, he showed them his hands and side. The disciples were overjoyed when they saw the Lord.

21 Again Jesus said, "Peace be with you! As the Father has sent me, I am sending you." 22 And with that he breathed on them and said, "Receive the Holy Spirit. 23 If you forgive anyone's sins, their sins are forgiven; if you do not forgive them, they are not forgiven."

Jesus Appears to Thomas

24 Now Thomas (also known as Didymus), one of the Twelve, was not with the disciples when Jesus came. 25 So the other disciples told him, "We have seen the Lord!"

But he said to them, "Unless I see the nail marks in his hands and put my finger where

The Resurrection of Jesus

the nails were, and put my hand into his side, I will not believe."

26 A week later his disciples were in the house again, and Thomas was with them. Though the doors were locked, Jesus came and stood among them and said, "Peace be with you!" 27 Then he said to Thomas, "Put your finger here; see my hands. Reach out your hand and put it into my side. Stop doubting and believe."

28 Thomas said to him, "My Lord and my God!"

29 Then Jesus told him, "Because you have seen me, you have believed; blessed are those who have not seen and yet have believed."

The Miraculous Catch of Fish

John 21:1 (NIV) Afterward Jesus appeared again to his disciples, by the Sea of Galilee. It happened this way: 2 Simon Peter, Thomas, Nathanael from Cana in Galilee, the sons of Zebedee, and two other disciples were together. 3 "I'm going out to fish," Simon Peter told them, and they said, "We'll go with you." So they went out and got into the boat, but that night they caught nothing.

4 Early in the morning, Jesus stood on the shore, but the disciples did not realize that it was Jesus.

5 He called out to them, "Friends, haven't you any fish?"

"No," they answered.

6 He said, "Throw your net on the right side of the boat and you will find some." When they did, they were unable to haul the net in

because of the large number of **fish**.

7 Then the disciple whom Jesus loved said to Peter, "It is the Lord!" As soon as Simon Peter heard him say, "It is the Lord," he wrapped his outer garment around him (for he had taken it off) and jumped into the water. 8 The other disciples followed in the boat, towing the net full of fish, for they were not far from shore, about a hundred yards. 9 When they landed, they saw a fire of burning coals there with fish on it, and some bread.

10 Jesus said to them, "Bring some of the fish you have just caught." 11 So Simon Peter climbed back into the boat and dragged the net ashore. It was full of large fish, but even with so many the net was not torn. 12 Jesus said to them, "Come and have breakfast." None of the disciples dared ask him, "Who are you?" They knew it was the Lord. 13 Jesus came, took the bread and gave it to them, and did the same with the fish. 14 This was now the third time Jesus appeared to his disciples after he was raised from the dead.

Jesus Reinstates Peter

15 When they had finished eating, Jesus said to Simon Peter, "Simon son of John, do you love me more than these?"

"Yes, Lord," he said, "you know that I love you."

Jesus said, "Feed my lambs."

16 Again Jesus said, "Simon son of John, do you love me?"

He answered, "Yes, Lord, you know that I

> *This same fish story occurs at the beginning of Jesus' ministry as well as here at the end. What does it mean?*

The Resurrection of Jesus

Jesus' three questions hurt Peter because he had denied knowing Jesus three times.

According to church history, Peter was eventually crucified.

love you."

Jesus said, "Take care of my sheep."

17 The third time he said to him, "Simon son of John, do you love me?"

Peter was **hurt** because Jesus asked him the third time, "Do you love me?" He said, "Lord, you know all things; you know that I love you."

Jesus said, "Feed my sheep. 18 Very truly I tell you, when you were younger you dressed yourself and went where you wanted; but when you are old you will stretch out your hands, and someone else will dress you and lead you where you do not want to go." 19 Jesus said this to indicate the kind of **death** by which Peter would glorify God. Then he said to him, "Follow me!"

20 Peter turned and saw that the disciple whom Jesus loved was following them. (This was the one who had leaned back against Jesus at the supper and had said, "Lord, who is going to betray you?") 21 When Peter saw him, he asked, "Lord, what about him?"

22 Jesus answered, "If I want him to remain alive until I return, what is that to you? You must follow me." 23 Because of this, the rumor spread among the believers that this disciple would not die. But Jesus did not say that he would not die; he only said, "If I want him to remain alive until I return, what is that to you?"

7. The Great Commission of Jesus

Matthew 28:16 (NRSV) Now the eleven disciples went to Galilee, to the mountain to which Jesus had directed them. 17 When they saw him, they worshiped him; but some doubted. 18 And Jesus came and said to them, "All authority in heaven and on earth has been given to me. 19 **Go** therefore and **make disciples** of all nations, **baptizing** them in the name of the Father and of the Son and of the Holy Spirit, 20 and **teaching** them to obey everything that I have commanded you. And remember, I am with you always, to the end of the age."

Simple: Go, make disciples— baptizing and teaching.

Mark 16:19 (NLT) When the Lord Jesus had finished talking with them, he was taken up into heaven and sat down in the place of honor at God's right hand. 20 And the disciples went everywhere and preached, and the Lord worked through them, confirming what they said by many miraculous signs.

The Purpose of John's Gospel

John 20:30 (NIV) Jesus performed many other signs in the presence of his disciples, which are not recorded in this book. 31 But these are written that **you may believe** that Jesus is the Messiah, the Son of God, and that by believing you may have life in his name.

This is the purpose of the Bible.

Part Two:
Jesus in Every Book of the Bible

1. The 5 Books of Moses

Genesis

3:15 (ESV) "I will put **enmity** between you and the woman, and between your offspring and her offspring; he shall bruise your head, and you shall bruise his heel."

Exodus

The Passover Lamb

12:21 (ESV) Then Moses called all the elders of Israel and said to them, "Go and select lambs for yourselves according to your clans, and kill the Passover *lamb*. 22 Take a bunch of **hyssop** and dip it in the blood that is in the basin, and touch the lintel and the two doorposts with the blood that is in the basin. None of you shall go out of the door of his house until the morning. 23 For the Lord will pass through to strike the Egyptians, and when he sees the blood on the lintel and on the two doorposts, the Lord will pass over the door and will not allow the destroyer to enter your houses to strike you.

The Manna

16:11 (ESV) And the Lord said to Moses, 12 "I have heard the grumbling of the people of Israel. Say to them, 'At twilight you shall eat meat, and **in the morning you shall be filled with bread**. Then you shall know that I am the Lord your God.'"

13 In the evening quail came up and covered the camp, and in the morning dew lay around

---

Jesus will ultimately crush Satan's head; but Satan will bruise His heel (make Jesus suffer on the cross).

Jesus was called "the lamb of God" at His baptism. John 1:29, pg. 13.

A sponge was dipped in wine vinegar and lifted up to Jesus on the cross on a stalk of hyssop—identifying Himself as the Passover lamb. John 19:28, pg. 91.

The 5 Books of Moses

Jesus talked about this event and then went on to say that He was the bread of life. John 6:32-34, pg. 37.

the camp. 14 And when the dew had gone up, there was on the face of the wilderness a fine, flake-like thing, fine as frost on the ground. 15 When the people of Israel saw it, they said to one another, "What is it?" (manna) For they did not know what it was. And Moses said to them, "**It is the bread that the Lord has given you to eat.**"

Leviticus

The Scapegoat

16:7 (ESV) Then he (Aaron the priest) shall take the two goats and set them before the Lord at the entrance of the tent of meeting. 8 And Aaron shall cast lots over the two goats, one lot for the Lord and the other lot for Azazel. 9 And Aaron shall present the goat on which the lot fell for the Lord and use it as a sin offering, 10 but the goat on which the lot fell for Azazel shall be presented alive before the Lord to make atonement over it, that it may be sent away into the wilderness to Azazel.

Jesus was the scapegoat taking the blame for our sin. He was both the sacrifice and the one sent away. He was crucified outside the city.

Numbers

Lifted Up

21:4 (ESV) From Mount Hor they set out by the way to the Red Sea, to go around the land of Edom. And the people became impatient on the way. 5 And the people spoke against God and against Moses, "Why have you brought us up out of Egypt to die in the wilderness? For there is no food and no water, and we loathe this worthless food." 6 Then the Lord sent fiery serpents among the people, and they bit the

Jesus used this story as a predictor of his death on

people, so that many people of Israel died. 7 And the people came to Moses and said, "We have sinned, for we have spoken against the Lord and against you. Pray to the Lord, that he take away the serpents from us." So Moses prayed for the people. 8 And the Lord said to Moses, "Make a fiery serpent and set it on a pole, and everyone who is bitten, when he sees it, shall live." 9 So Moses made a **bronze serpent** and set it on a pole. And if a serpent bit anyone, he would look at the bronze serpent and live.

> the cross. John 3:14-18, pg. 17.
>
> In trouble today? Don't know where to turn? I need to look up. Keep my eyes on Jesus.

Deuteronomy

A New Prophet like Moses

18:15 (ESV) "The Lord your God will raise up for you a prophet like me from among you, from your brothers—it is to him you shall listen—16 just as you desired of the Lord your God at Horeb on the day of the assembly, when you said, 'Let me not hear again the voice of the Lord my God or see this great fire any more, lest I die.' 17 And the Lord said to me, 'They are right in what they have spoken. 18 ***I will raise up for them a prophet like you from among their brothers.*** And I will put my words in his mouth, and he shall speak to them all that I command him. 19 And whoever will not listen to my words that he shall speak in my name, I myself will require it of him.

> Jesus is a prophet like Moses—the one who saves his people.

2. The 12 Historical Books

Joshua

The Commander of the Lord's Army

Many think this was Jesus. Who else could it be?

This happened only one other time—when God spoke to Moses out of the burning bush.

Like Sarah, Rebekah, and ultimately Mary, Jesus' mother.

Samson becomes a type of Christ—one who saves his people.

15:13 (ESV) When Joshua was by Jericho, he lifted up his eyes and looked, and behold, a man was standing before him with his drawn sword in his hand. And Joshua went to him and said to him, "Are you for us, or for our adversaries?" 14 And he said, "No; but **I am the commander of the army of the Lord**. Now I have come." And Joshua fell on his face to the earth and worshiped and said to him, "What does my lord say to his servant?" 15 And the commander of the Lord's army said to Joshua, "**Take off your sandals** from your feet, for the place where you are standing is holy." And Joshua did so.

Judges

13:2 (ESV) There was a certain man of Zorah, of the tribe of the Danites, whose name was Manoah. And his wife was **barren** and had no children. 3 And the **angel of the Lord appeared** to the woman and said to her, "Behold, you are barren and have not borne children, but you shall conceive and bear a son... 5 and he shall begin to save Israel from the hand of the Philistines... 24 And the woman bore a son and called his name **Samson**. And the young man grew, and the Lord blessed him. 25 And the Spirit of the Lord began to stir him in ....

Ruth

The Kinsman Redeemer

4:9 (ESV) Then Boaz said to the elders and all the people, "You are witnesses this day that I have bought from the hand of Naomi all that belonged to Elimelech and all that belonged to Chilion and to Mahlon. 10 Also Ruth the Moabite, the widow of Mahlon, I have bought to be my wife, to perpetuate the name of the dead in his inheritance, that the name of the dead may not be cut off from among his brothers and from the gate of his native place. You are witnesses this day." 11 Then all the people who were at the gate and the elders said, "We are witnesses. May the Lord make the woman, who is coming into your house, like Rachel and Leah, who together built up the house of Israel. May you act worthily in Ephrathah and be renowned in Bethlehem, 12 and may your house be like the house of Perez, whom Tamar bore to Judah, because of the offspring that the Lord will give you by this young woman."

13 So Boaz took Ruth, and she became his wife. And he went in to her, and the Lord gave her conception, and she bore a son. 14 Then the women said to Naomi, "Blessed be the Lord, who has not left you this day without a redeemer, and may his name be renowned in Israel! 15 He shall be to you **a restorer of life** and a nourisher of your old age, for your daughter-in-law who loves you, who is more to you than seven sons, has given birth to him." 16 Then Naomi took the child and laid him on her lap and became his nurse. 17 And the women of the neighborhood gave him a

---

Naomi would've lost her family's land if a relative hadn't stepped in. Boaz, the kinsman redeemer, saved the land by marrying Ruth. Jesus is my kinsman redeemer.

This is the mission of Jesus.

The 12 Historical Books

Jesus was of the line and lineage of King David. Luke 2:4, pg 8.

name, saying, "A son has been born to Naomi." They named him Obed. He was the father of Jesse, the father of **David**...

1 & 2 Samuel

David's Throne

2 Samuel 7:12 (ESV) When your days are fulfilled and you lie down with your fathers, I will raise up your offspring after you, who shall come from your body, and I will establish his (David's son, Solomon) kingdom. 13 He shall build a house (the temple) for my name, and I will establish the throne of his kingdom forever. 14 I will be to him a father, and he shall be to me a son. When he commits iniquity, I will discipline him with the rod of men, with the stripes of the sons of men, 15 but my steadfast love will not depart from him, as I took it from Saul, whom I put away from before you. 16 And your house and your kingdom shall be made sure forever before me. **Your throne shall be established forever**.

God is speaking to King David at the end of his life.

This is ultimately Jesus, the long-awaited son who would inherit the throne of David.

1 & 2 Kings

Bread Multiplied

2 Kings 4:42 (ESV) A man came from Baal-shalishah, bringing the man of God bread of the firstfruits, twenty loaves of barley and fresh ears of grain in his sack. And Elisha said, "Give to the men, that they may eat." 43 But his servant said, "How can I set this before a hundred men?" So he repeated, "Give them to the men, that they may eat, for thus says the Lord, 'They shall eat and have some left.'" 44

Jesus does this same miracle hundreds of years later, feeding not just 100, but 5000. Luke 9, pg. 69.

So he set it before them. And they ate and had some left, according to the word of the Lord.

1 & 2 Chronicles

2 Chronicles 6:13 (ESV) Solomon ... knelt on his knees in the presence of all the assembly of Israel, and spread out his hands toward heaven, 14 and said, "O Lord, God of Israel, there is no God like you, in heaven or on earth, keeping covenant and showing steadfast love to your servants who walk before you with all their heart, 15 who have kept with your servant David my father what you declared to him. You spoke with your mouth, and with your hand have fulfilled it this day. 16 Now therefore, O Lord, God of Israel, keep for your servant David my father what you have promised him, saying, 'You shall not lack a man to sit before me on the throne of Israel, if only your sons pay close attention to their way, to walk in my law as you have walked before me.' 17 Now therefore, O Lord, God of Israel, let your word be confirmed, which you have spoken to your servant David.

18 "But will **God** indeed **dwell with man** on the earth? Behold, heaven and the highest heaven cannot contain you, how much less this house that I have built! 19 Yet have regard to the prayer of your servant and to his plea, O Lord my God, listening to the cry and to the prayer that your servant prays before you, 20 that your eyes may be open day and night toward this house, the place where you have promised to set your name, that you may listen to the prayer that your servant offers to-

John 1:14 "The Word became flesh and made his dwelling among us" (pg 4).

Ezra

Passover Celebrated

6:19 (ESV) On the fourteenth day of the first month, the returned exiles kept the Passover. 20 For the priests and the Levites had purified themselves together; all of them were clean. So they slaughtered the **Passover lamb** for all the returned exiles, for their fellow priests, and for themselves. 21 It was eaten by the people of Israel who had returned from exile, and also by every one who had joined them and separated himself from the uncleanness of the peoples of the land to worship the Lord, the God of Israel.

Nehemiah

9:5 (ESV) Then the Levites, **Jeshua**, Kadmiel, Bani, Hashabneiah, Sherebiah, Hodiah, Shebaniah, and Pethahiah, said, "Stand up and bless the Lord your God from everlasting to everlasting. Blessed be your glorious name, which is exalted above all blessing and praise. 6 You are the Lord, you alone. You have made heaven, the heaven of heavens, with all their host, the earth and all that is on it, the seas and all that is in them; and you preserve all of them; and the host of heaven worships you.

Margin notes:

ward this place. 21 And listen to the pleas of your servant and of your people Israel, when they pray toward this place. And listen from heaven your dwelling place, and when you hear, forgive.

The Passover celebrated God's salvation in the past, but more importantly God's coming salvation, the real Passover lamb—Jesus.

Jeshua is the Hebrew name for Jesus.

Esther

4:12 (ESV) And they told Mordecai what Esther had said. 13 Then Mordecai told them to reply to Esther, "Do not think to yourself that in the king's palace you will escape any more than all the other Jews. 14 For if you keep silent at this time, relief and deliverance will rise for the Jews from another place, but you and your father's house will perish. And who knows whether you have not come to the kingdom for such a time as this?" 15 Then Esther told them to reply to Mordecai, 16 "Go, gather all the Jews to be found in Susa, and hold a fast on my behalf, and do not eat or drink for three days, night or day. I and my young women will also fast as you do. Then I will go to the king, though it is against the law, and **if I perish, I perish**."

> God saves his people through a redeemer—someone who is willing to die for his or her people (i.e. Jesus)!

3. The 5 Poetic Books

Job

The Redeemer

19:25 (ESV) For I know that **my Redeemer lives**, and at the last he will stand upon the earth. 26 And after my skin has been thus destroyed, yet in my flesh I shall see God, 27 whom I shall see for myself, and my eyes shall behold, and not another. My heart faints within me!

Psalms

Suffering One

22:1 (ESV) **My God, my God, why have you forsaken me?** Why are you so far from saving me, from the words of my groaning?

14 I am poured out like water, and all my bones are out of joint; my heart is like wax; it is melted within my breast; 15 my strength is dried up like a potsherd, and my tongue sticks to my jaws; you lay me in the dust of death. 16 For dogs encompass me; a company of evildoers encircles me; they have **pierced my hands and feet**. I can count all my bones— they stare and gloat over me; 18 **they divide my garments among them**, and for my clothing they cast lots.

The Lord Is My Shepherd

23:1 (ESV) The Lord is my **shepherd**; I shall not want. 2 He makes me lie down in green pastures. He leads me beside still waters. 3 He

---

Job had faith in Jesus, even though he didn't know Him. I want that kind of faith.

Jesus' fourth word from the cross. Mark 15:34, pg. 91.

Jesus was nailed to the cross by His hands and feet.

John 19:23-24; pg. 90.

Jesus said, "I am the good shepherd.

restores my soul. He leads me in paths of righteousness for his name's sake. 4 Even though I walk through the valley of the shadow of death, I will fear no evil, for you are with me; your rod and your staff, they comfort me. 5 You prepare a table before me in the presence of my enemies; you anoint my head with oil; my cup overflows. 6 Surely goodness and mercy shall follow me all the days of my life, and I shall dwell in the house of the Lord forever.

> The good shepherd lays down his life for the sheep." John 10:11; pg. 41.

Proverbs

Son of God

30:4 (ESV) Who has ascended to heaven and come down? Who has gathered the wind in his fists? Who has wrapped up the waters in a garment? Who has established all the ends of the earth? What is his name, and **what is his son's name**? Surely you know!

> Jesus!

Ecclesiastes

4:7 (ESV) I saw vanity under the sun: 8 one person who has no other, either son or brother, yet there is no end to all his toil, and his eyes are never satisfied with riches, so that he never asks, "For whom am I toiling and depriving myself of pleasure?" This also is vanity and an unhappy business. 9 Two are better than one, because they have a good reward for their toil. 10 For if they fall, one will lift up his fellow. But woe to him who is alone when he falls and has not another to lift him up! 11 Again, if two lie together, they keep warm, but how can one keep warm alone? 12 And though a man might prevail against one who is alone,

The 5 Poetic Books

Newlyweds often quote this verse at their wedding:
1. Man
2. Woman
3. Jesus

Jesus loves me so much that He died for me.

two will withstand him—a **threefold** cord is not quickly broken.

Song of Solomon

8:6 (ESV) Set me as a seal upon your heart, as a seal upon your arm, for **love is strong as death**, jealousy is fierce as the grave. Its flashes are flashes of fire, the very flame of the Lord.

4. The 5 Major Prophets

Isaiah

Virgin Born & Emmanuel

7:14 (ESV) Therefore the Lord himself will give you a sign. Behold, the **virgin** shall conceive and bear a **son**, and shall call his name Immanuel (meaning "God with us").

> The virgin - Mary. The son - Jesus. Matthew 1:23, pg 8.

Our Peace

9:6 (ESV) For to us a child is born, to us a son is given; and the government shall be upon his shoulder, and his name shall be called Wonderful Counselor, Mighty God, Everlasting Father, Prince of **Peace**.

> At Jesus' birth the angels sang "...peace among men with whom He is pleased." Luke 2:14, pg 9.

Suffering Savior

53:1 (ESV) Who has believed what he has heard from us? And to whom has the arm of the Lord been revealed? 2 For he grew up before him like a young plant, and like a root out of dry ground; he had no form or majesty that we should look at him, and no beauty that we should desire him. 3 He was despised and rejected by men; a man of sorrows, and acquainted with grief; and as one from whom men hide their faces he was despised, and we esteemed him not. 4 Surely he has borne our griefs and carried our sorrows; yet we esteemed him stricken, smitten by God, and afflicted. 5 But he was **pierced** for our transgressions; he was crushed for our iniquities; upon him was the chastisement that brought us peace, and with his wounds we are healed. 6 All we like sheep have gone astray; we have

> John 19:34, pg. 93.

The 5 Major Prophets

Mark 14:61, pg. 83.

turned—every one—to his own way; and the Lord has laid on him the iniquity of us all. 7 He was oppressed, and he was afflicted, yet he opened not his mouth; like a lamb that is led to the slaughter, and like a sheep that before its shearers is **silent, so he opened not his mouth.** 8 By oppression and judgment he was taken away; and as for his generation, who considered that he was cut off out of the land of the living, stricken for the transgression of my people? 9 And they made his grave with the wicked and with a rich man in his death, although he had done no violence, and there was no deceit in his mouth. 10 Yet it was the will of the Lord to crush him; he has put him to grief; when his soul makes an offering for guilt, he shall see his offspring; he shall prolong his days; the will of the Lord shall prosper in his hand. 11 Out of the anguish of his soul he shall see and be satisfied; by his knowledge shall the righteous one, my servant, make many to be accounted righteous, and he shall bear their iniquities. 12 Therefore I will divide him a portion with the many, and he shall divide the spoil with the strong, because he poured out his soul to death and was numbered with the transgressors; yet he bore the sin of many, and makes intercession for the transgressors.

Jeremiah

30:1 (ESV) The word that came to Jeremiah from the Lord: 2 "Thus says the Lord, the God of Israel: Write in a book all the words that I have spoken to you. 3 For behold, days are coming, declares the Lord, when I will restore the fortunes of my people, Israel and Judah, says the Lord, and I will bring them back to the land that I gave to their fathers, and they shall take possession of it." 4 These are the words that the Lord spoke concerning Israel and Judah: 5 "Thus says the Lord: We have heard a cry of panic, of terror, and no peace. 6 Ask now, and see, can a man bear a child? Why then do I see every man with his hands on his stomach like a woman in labor? Why has every face turned pale? 7 Alas! That day is so great there is none like it; it is a time of distress for Jacob; yet he shall be saved out of it. 8 "And it shall come to pass in that day, declares the Lord of hosts, that I will break his yoke from off your neck, and I will burst your bonds, and foreigners shall no more make a servant of him. 9 But they shall serve the Lord their God and David their king, whom I will raise up for them. 10 "Then fear not, O Jacob my servant, declares the Lord, nor be dismayed, O Israel; for behold, I will save you from far away, and your offspring from the land of their captivity. Jacob shall return and have quiet and ease, and none shall make him afraid. 11 **For I am with you to save you, declares the Lord** ....

This is a description of Jesus—He is "with me to save me."

Lamentations

Restore Us to Yourself, O Lord

5:1 (ESV) Remember, O Lord, what has befallen us; look, and see our disgrace! 15 The joy of our hearts has ceased; our dancing has been turned to mourning. 16 The crown has fallen from our head; woe to us, for we have sinned! 17 For this our heart has become sick, for these things our eyes have grown dim,

18 for Mount Zion which lies desolate; jackals prowl over it. 19 But you, O Lord, reign forever; your throne endures to all generations.

20 Why do you forget us forever, why do you forsake us for so many days? 21 **Restore us to yourself, O Lord**, that we may be restored! Renew our days as of old—22 unless you have utterly rejected us, and you remain exceedingly angry with us.

Ezekiel

34:11 (ESV) "For thus says the Lord God: Behold, I, myself will search for my sheep and will seek them out. 12 As a shepherd seeks out his flock when he is among his sheep that have been scattered, so will I seek out my sheep, and I will rescue them from all places where they have been scattered on a day of clouds and thick darkness. 13 And I will bring them out from the peoples and gather them from the countries, and will bring them into their own land. And I will feed them on the mountains of Israel, by the ravines, and in all the inhabited places of the country. 14 I will feed them with good pasture, and on the mountain heights of Israel shall be their grazing land. There they shall lie down in good grazing land, and on rich pasture they shall feed on the mountains of Israel. 15 I myself will be the shepherd of my sheep, and I myself will make them lie down, declares the Lord God. 16 I will seek the lost, and I will bring back the strayed, and I will bind up the injured, and I will strengthen the weak, and the fat and the strong I will destroy. I will feed them in justice.

This is the heart of Jesus' mission on earth.

17 "As for you, my flock, thus says the Lord God: Behold, I judge between sheep and sheep, between rams and male goats. 18 Is it not enough for you to feed on the good pasture, that you must tread down with your feet the rest of your pasture; and to drink of clear water, that you must muddy the rest of the water with your feet? 19 And must my sheep eat what you have trodden with your feet, and drink what you have muddied with your feet?

20 "Therefore, thus says the Lord God to them: Behold, I, I myself will judge between the fat sheep and the lean sheep. 21 Because you push with side and shoulder, and thrust at all the weak with your horns, till you have scattered them abroad, 22 I will rescue my flock; they shall no longer be a prey. And I will judge between sheep and sheep. 23 **And I will set up over them one shepherd, my servant David, and he shall feed them: he shall feed them and be their shepherd.** 24 And I, the Lord, will be their God, and my servant David shall be prince among them. I am the Lord; I have spoken.

The Lord's Covenant of Peace

25 "I will make with them a covenant of peace and banish wild beasts from the land, so that they may dwell securely in the wilderness and sleep in the woods. 26 And I will make them and the places all around my hill a blessing, and I will send down the showers in their season; they shall be showers of blessing. 27 And the trees of the field shall yield their fruit, and the earth shall yield its increase, and they shall be secure in their land.

David was a shepherd, but the prophet Ezekiel is not talking about David. He had already died. Ezekiel is talking about the son of David— Jesus.

And they shall know that I am the Lord, when I break the bars of their yoke, and deliver them from the hand of those who enslaved them. 28 They shall no more be a prey to the nations, nor shall the beasts of the land devour them. They shall dwell securely, and none shall make them afraid. 29 And I will provide for them renowned plantations so that they shall no more be consumed with hunger in the land, and no longer suffer the reproach of the nations. 30 And they shall know that I am the Lord their God with them, and that they, the house of Israel, are my people, declares the Lord God. 31 And **you are my sheep, human sheep of my pasture, and I am your God**, declares the Lord God."

John 10:14
pg. 41.

Daniel

The Son of the Gods

3:1 (ESV) King Nebuchadnezzar made an image of gold, whose height was sixty cubits and its breadth six cubits. He set it up on the plain of Dura, in the province of Babylon. 2 Then King Nebuchadnezzar sent to gather the satraps, the prefects, and the governors, the counselors, the treasurers, the justices, the magistrates, and all the officials of the provinces to come to the dedication of the image that King Nebuchadnezzar had set up. 3 Then the satraps, the prefects, and the governors, the counselors, the treasurers, the justices, the magistrates, and all the officials of the provinces gathered for the dedication of the image that King Nebuchadnezzar had set up. And they stood before the image that Nebuchadnezzar had set up. 4 And the herald proclaimed aloud, "You are commanded, O peoples, nations, and languages, 5 that when you hear the sound of the horn, pipe, lyre, trigon, harp, bagpipe, and every kind of music, you are to fall down and worship the golden image that King Nebuchadnezzar has set up. 6 And whoever does not fall down and worship shall immediately be cast into a burning fiery furnace." 7 Therefore, as soon as all the peoples heard the sound of the horn, pipe, lyre, trigon, harp, bagpipe, and every kind of music, all the peoples, nations, and languages fell down and worshiped the golden image that King Nebuchadnezzar had set up.

The Fiery Furnace

8 Therefore at that time certain Chaldeans came forward and maliciously accused the Jews. 9 They declared to King Nebuchadnezzar, "O king, live forever! 10 You, O king, have made a decree, that every man who hears the sound of the horn, pipe, lyre, trigon, harp, bagpipe, and every kind of music, shall fall down and worship the golden image. 11 And whoever does not fall down and worship shall be cast into a burning fiery furnace. 12 There are certain Jews whom you have appointed over the affairs of the province of Babylon: Shadrach, Meshach, and Abednego. These men, O king, pay no attention to you; they do not serve your gods or worship the golden image that you have set up."

13 Then Nebuchadnezzar in furious rage commanded that Shadrach, Meshach, and Abednego be brought. So they brought

these men before the king. 14 Nebuchadnezzar answered and said to them, "Is it true, O Shadrach, Meshach, and Abednego, that you do not serve my gods or worship the golden image that I have set up? 15 Now if you are ready when you hear the sound of the horn, pipe, lyre, trigon, harp, bagpipe, and every kind of music, to fall down and worship the image that I have made, well and good. But if you do not worship, you shall immediately be cast into a burning fiery furnace. And who is the god who will deliver you out of my hands?"

16 Shadrach, Meshach, and Abednego answered and said to the king, "O Nebuchadnezzar, we have no need to answer you in this matter. 17 If this be so, our God whom we serve is able to deliver us from the burning fiery furnace, and he will deliver us out of your hand, O king. 18 But if not, be it known to you, O king, that we will not serve your gods or worship the golden image that you have set up."

19 Then Nebuchadnezzar was filled with fury, and the expression of his face was changed against Shadrach, Meshach, and Abednego. He ordered the furnace heated seven times more than it was usually heated. 20 And he ordered some of the mighty men of his army to bind Shadrach, Meshach, and Abednego, and to cast them into the burning fiery furnace. 21 Then these men were (bound in their cloaks, their tunics, their hats, and their other garments, and they were thrown into the burning fiery furnace. 22 Because the king's order was urgent and the furnace overheated, the flame of the fire killed those men who took up Shadrach, Meshach, and Abednego.

23 And these three men, Shadrach, Meshach, and Abednego, fell bound into the burning fiery furnace.

24 Then King Nebuchadnezzar was astonished and rose up in haste. He declared to his counselors, "Did we not cast three men bound into the fire?" They answered and said to the king, "True, O king." 25 He answered and said, "But I see four men unbound, walking in the midst of the fire, and they are not hurt; and the **appearance of the fourth is like a son of the gods**."

Could this strange, mysterious fourth person be Jesus?

26 Then Nebuchadnezzar came near to the door of the burning fiery furnace; he declared, "Shadrach, Meshach, and Abednego, servants of the Most High God, come out, and come here!" Then Shadrach, Meshach, and Abednego came out from the fire. 27 And the satraps, the prefects, the governors, and the king's counselors gathered together and saw that the fire had not had any power over the bodies of those men. The hair of their heads was not singed, their cloaks were not harmed, and no smell of fire had come upon them. 28 Nebuchadnezzar answered and said, "Blessed be the God of Shadrach, Meshach, and Abednego, who has sent his angel and **delivered his servants, who trusted in him**, and set aside the king's command, and yielded up their bodies rather than serve and worship any god except their own God. 29 Therefore I make a decree: Any people, nation, or language that speaks anything against the God of Shadrach, Meshach, and Abednego shall be torn limb from limb, and their houses laid in ruins, for there is no other god who is able to

To what or to whom am I going to trust my life?

The 5 Major Prophets

[Margin note: Jesus again?]

rescue in this way." 30 Then the king promoted Shadrach, Meshach, and Abednego in the province of Babylon.

Son of Man

7:13 (ESV) "I saw in the night visions, and behold, with the clouds of heaven there came one like a **son of man**, and he came to the Ancient of Days and was presented before him. 14 And to him was given dominion and glory and a kingdom, that all peoples, nations, and languages should serve him; his dominion is an everlasting dominion, which shall not pass away, and his kingdom one that shall not be destroyed.

5. The 12 Minor Prophets

Hosea

The Lord's Love for Israel

11:1 (ESV) When Israel was a child, I loved him, and out of Egypt *I called my son*.

Joel

2:18 (ESV) Then the Lord became jealous for his land and had pity on his people. 19 The Lord answered and said to his people, "Behold, I am sending to you grain, wine, and oil, and you will be satisfied; and I will no more make you a reproach among the nations. 20 "I will remove the northerner far from you, and drive him into a parched and desolate land, his vanguard into the eastern sea, and his rear guard into the western sea; the stench and foul smell of him will rise, for he has done great things. 21 "Fear not, O land; be glad and rejoice, for the Lord has done great things! 22 Fear not, you beasts of the field, for the pastures of the wilderness are green; the tree bears its fruit; the fig tree and vine give their full yield. 23 "Be glad, O children of Zion, and rejoice in the Lord your God, for he has given the early rain for your vindication; he has poured down for you abundant rain, the early and the latter rain, as before. 24 "The threshing floors shall be full of grain; the vats shall overflow with wine and oil. 25 I will restore to you the years that the swarming locust has eaten, the hopper, the destroyer, and the cutter, my great army, which I sent among you.

> Jesus too was called out of Egypt as a young boy.

26 "You shall eat in plenty and be satisfied, and praise the name of the Lord your God, who has dealt wondrously with you. And my people shall never again be put to shame. 27 You shall know that I am in the midst of Israel, and that I am the Lord your God and there is none else. And my people shall never again be put to shame.

The Lord Will Pour Out His Spirit

28 "And it shall come to pass afterward, that I will pour out my Spirit on all flesh; your sons and your daughters shall prophesy, your old men shall dream dreams, and your young men shall see visions. 29 Even on the male and female servants in those days I will pour out my Spirit. 30 "And I will show wonders in the heavens and on the earth, blood and fire and columns of smoke. 31 **The sun shall be turned to darkness, and the moon to blood, before the great and awesome day of the Lord comes.** 32 And it shall come to pass that everyone who calls on the name of the Lord shall be saved.

Amos

The Restoration of Israel

9:11 (ESV) "In that day I will raise up the **booth of David** that is fallen and repair its breaches, and raise up its ruins and rebuild it as in the days of old, 12 that they may possess the remnant of Edom and all the nations who are called by my name," declares the Lord who does this. 13 "Behold, the days are coming," declares the Lord, "when the plow-

Jesus quoted these words hundreds of years later. They describe his second coming.

Jesus is of the "booth of David" and he ultimately will restore His people.

man shall overtake the reaper and the treader of grapes him who sows the seed; the mountains shall drip sweet wine, and all the hills shall flow with it. 14 I will restore the fortunes of my people Israel, and they shall rebuild the ruined cities and inhabit them; they shall plant vineyards and drink their wine, and they shall make gardens and eat their fruit. 15 I will plant them on their land, and they shall never again be uprooted out of the land that I have given them," says the Lord your God.

Obadiah

1:17 (ESV) But in Mount Zion there shall be **those who escape, and it shall be holy, and the house of Jacob shall possess their own possessions**.

Jonah

1:1 (ESV) The word of the Lord came to Jonah son of Amittai: 2 "Go to the great city of Nineveh and preach against it, because its wickedness has come up before me." 3 But Jonah ran away from the Lord and headed for Tarshish. He went down to Joppa, where he found a ship bound for that port. After paying the fare, he went aboard and sailed for Tarshish to flee from the Lord.

4 Then the Lord sent a great wind on the sea, and such a violent storm arose that the ship threatened to break up. 5 All the sailors were afraid and each cried out to his own god. And they threw the cargo into the sea to lighten the ship. But Jonah had gone below deck, where he lay down and fell into a deep sleep.

> Obadiah, in the midst of the total destruction of Israel, predicts there will be a remnant. And out of that remnant would come a savior—Jesus.

6 The captain went to him and said, "How can you sleep? Get up and call on your god! Maybe he will take notice of us, and we will not perish."

7 Then the sailors said to each other, "Come, let us cast lots to find out who is responsible for this calamity." They cast lots and the lot fell on Jonah.

8 So they asked him, "Tell us, who is responsible for making all this trouble for us? What do you do? Where do you come from? What is your country? From what people are you?"

9 He answered, "I am a Hebrew and I worship the Lord , the God of heaven, who made the sea and the land." 10 This terrified them and they asked, "What have you done?" (They knew he was running away from the Lord, because he had already told them so.) 11 The sea was getting rougher and rougher. So they asked him, "What should we do to you to make the sea calm down for us?" 12 "Pick me up and throw me into the sea," he replied, "and it will become calm. I know that it is my fault that this great storm has come upon you." 13 Instead, the men did their best to row back to land. But they could not, for the sea grew even wilder than before.14 Then they cried to the Lord, "O Lord, please do not let us die for taking this man's life. Do not hold us accountable for killing an innocent man, for you, O Lord, have done as you pleased." 15 Then they took Jonah and threw him overboard, and the raging sea grew calm.

16 At this the men greatly feared the Lord, and they offered a sacrifice to the Lord and

made vows to him.

17 But the Lord provided a great fish to swallow Jonah, and Jonah was inside the fish **three days and three nights**.

Micah

5:2 (ESV) But you, O **Bethlehem** Ephrathah, who are too little to be among the clans of Judah, from you shall come forth for me one who is to be ruler in Israel, whose coming forth is from of old, from ancient days.

Nahum

1:15 (ESV) **Behold, upon the mountains, the feet of him who brings good news**, who publishes peace. Keep your feasts, O Judah; fulfill your vows, for never again shall the worthless pass through you: he is utterly cut off.

Habakkuk

Habakkuk Rejoices in the Lord

3:17 (ESV) Though the fig tree should not blossom, nor fruit be on the vines, the produce of the olive fail and the fields yield no food, the flock be cut off from the fold and there be no herd in the stalls, 18 yet *I will rejoice in the Lord; I will take joy in the God of my salvation*. 19 God, the Lord, is my strength; he makes my feet like the deer's; he makes me tread on my high places.

Jesus predicted his grave stay with this verse.

This is the prophecy of Jesus birth. Matthew 2:5, pg 12.

Isaiah said these words (52:7). So did Paul (Romans 10:15). Both were talking about Jesus.

John 18, pg. 80.

Zephaniah

Israel's Joy and Restoration

3:14 (ESV) Sing aloud, O daughter of Zion: shout, O Israel! Rejoice and exult with all your heart, O daughter of Jerusalem! 15 The Lord has taken away the judgments against you; he has cleared away your enemies. The King of Israel, **the Lord, is in your midst**; you shall never again fear evil. 16 On that day it shall be said to Jerusalem: "Fear not, O Zion; let not your hands grow weak. 17 The Lord **your God is in your midst, a mighty one who will save**: he will rejoice over you with gladness; he will quiet you by his love; he will exult over you with loud singing. 18 I will gather those of you who mourn for the festival, so that you will no longer suffer reproach. 19 Behold, at that time I will deal with all your oppressors. And I will save the lame and gather the outcast, and I will change their shame into praise and renown in all the earth. 20 At that time I will bring you in, at the time when I gather you together; for I will make you renowned and praised among all the peoples of the earth, when I restore your fortunes before your eyes," says the Lord.

Sounds like Jesus.

Haggai

The Coming Glory of the Temple

2:1 (ESV) In the seventh month, on the twenty-first day of the month, the word of the Lord came by the hand of Haggai the prophet, 2 "Speak now to Zerubbabel the son of Shealtiel, governor of Judah, and to Joshua the

The people of Israel returned from exile and began rebuilding the temple... But soon they quit—for 18 years. The temple was finally rebuilt under

son of Jehozadak, the high priest, and to all the remnant of the people, and say, 3 'Who is left among you who saw this house in its former glory? How do you see it now? Is it not as nothing in your eyes? 4 Yet now be strong, O Zerubbabel, declares the Lord. Be strong, O Joshua, son of Jehozadak, the high priest. Be strong, all you people of the land, declares the Lord. Work, for I am with you, declares the Lord of hosts, 5 according to the covenant that I made with you when you came out of Egypt. My Spirit remains in your midst. Fear not. 6 For thus says the Lord of hosts: Yet once more, in a little while, I will shake the heavens and the earth and the sea and the dry land. 7 And I will shake all nations, so that the treasures of all nations shall come in, and I will fill this house with glory, says the Lord of hosts. 8 **The silver is mine**, and the **gold is mine**, declares the Lord of hosts. 9 The latter glory of this house shall be greater than the former, says the Lord of hosts. And in this place I will give peace, declares the Lord of hosts.'"

Zechariah

The Coming King of Zion

9:9 (ESV) Rejoice greatly, O daughter of Zion! Shout aloud, O daughter of Jerusalem! Behold, your king is coming to you; righteous and having salvation is he, humble and mounted on a **donkey**, on a colt, the foal of a donkey.

11:12 (ESV) Then I said to them, "If it seems good to you, give me my wages; but if not, keep them." And they weighed out as my wages **thirty pieces of silver**. 13 Then the

---

the prophet Haggai; it was the symbol of God living among his people.

Later Jesus became the living temple —the living presence of God.

Jesus, hundreds of years later, cleared out the money changers in the Temple.

Christians celebrate Jesus' fulfillment of this event on Palm Sunday. See John 12:15, pg. 75.

Judas

The 12 Minor Prophets

was paid 30 pieces of silver to betray Jesus. The money was used to buy a potter's field. Matt. 27:9, 10; pg. 85.

The prophet Malachi looks forward to the story of John's birth (including a reference to Elijah). John becomes the messenger who prepares the way for the Messiah (Luke 1).

Lord said to me, "Throw it to the potter"—the lordly price at which I was priced by them. So I took the thirty pieces of silver and threw them into the house of the Lord, to the potter.

Malachi

3:1 (ESV) "Behold, I send my messenger, and he will prepare the way before me. And the **Lord whom you seek** will suddenly come to his temple; and the messenger of the covenant in whom you delight, behold, he is coming, says the Lord of hosts.

4:5 (ESV) "Behold, I will send you **Elijah** the prophet before the great and awesome day of the Lord comes.

6. The 4 Gospels
See Part 1.

7. The Book of Acts

4:11 (ESV) This Jesus is the stone that was rejected by you, the builders, which has become the cornerstone. 12 And there is salvation in no one else, for there is no other name under heaven given among men by which we must be **saved**.

> Jesus is the Savior. What do I need saving from?

8. The Letters

Romans

6:23 (ESV) For the wages of sin is death, but the **free gift** of God is eternal life in Christ Jesus our Lord.

Jesus paid the price so you I don't have to.

1 Corinthians

15:51 (ESV) Behold! I tell you a mystery. We shall not all sleep, but we shall all be changed, 52 in a moment, in the twinkling of an eye, at the last trumpet. For the trumpet will sound, and the dead will be raised imperishable, and we shall be changed. 53 For this perishable body must put on the imperishable, and this mortal body must put on immortality. 54 When the perishable puts on the imperishable, and the mortal puts on immortality, then shall come to pass the saying that is written:

There is one enemy that I can not defeat on my own - death. I need the victory that Jesus won for me by dying on the cross and rising from the dead on the third day.

"Death is swallowed up in victory." 55 "O death, **where is your victory**? O death, where is your sting?" 56 The sting of death is sin, and the power of sin is the law. 57 But thanks be to God, who gives us the **victory through our Lord Jesus Christ**. 58 Therefore, my beloved brothers, be steadfast, immovable, always abounding in the work of the Lord, knowing that in the Lord your labor is not in vain.

2 Corinthians

5:17 (ESV) Therefore, if anyone is **in Christ**, he is **a new creation**. The old has passed away; behold, the new has come. 18 All this is from God, who through Christ reconciled us

Good news. In Christ, I can become

to himself and gave us the ministry of reconciliation; 19 that is, in Christ God was reconciling the world to himself, not counting their trespasses against them, and entrusting to us the message of reconciliation. 20 Therefore, we are ambassadors for Christ, God making his appeal through us. We implore you on behalf of Christ, be reconciled to God. 21 For our sake he made him to be sin who knew no sin, so that in him we might become the righteousness of God.

something new!

Galatians

5:22 (ESV) But the fruit of the Spirit is love, joy, peace, patience, kindness, goodness, faithfulness, 23 gentleness, self-control; against such things there is no law. 24 And those who **belong to Christ Jesus** have crucified the flesh with its passions and desires.

25 If we live by the Spirit, let us also keep in step with the Spirit. 26 Let us not become conceited, provoking one another, envying one another.

Jesus was not the only thing on the cross—my sins were nailed there as well.

Ephesians

2:8 (ESV) For by grace you have been saved through faith. And this is not your own doing; it is the gift of God, 9 not a result of works, so that no one may boast. 10 For we are his **workmanship, created in Christ Jesus** for good works, which God prepared beforehand, that we should walk in them.

3:16 (ESV) that according to the riches of his glory he may grant you to be strengthened with power through his Spirit in your in-

The word "workmanship" literally means "poem" or "art."

The Letters

I may feel alone, rejected, and unloved, but God's love for me in Christ knows no boundaries.

God wants more for me than I do.

I can climb my way to the top and end up alone, fearful of falling. Or I can follow Jesus' example—be humble and let Jesus lift me up.

ner being, 17 so that Christ may dwell in your hearts through faith—that you, being rooted and grounded in love, 18 may have strength to comprehend with all the saints what is the breadth and length and height and depth, 19 and to know the **love of Christ** that surpasses knowledge, that you may be filled with all the fullness of God. 20 Now to him who is able to do far **more abundantly** than all that we ask or think, according to the power at work within us, 21 to him be glory in the church and in Christ Jesus throughout all generations, forever and ever. Amen.

Philippians

2:5 (ESV) Have this mind among yourselves, which is yours in Christ Jesus, 6 who, though he was in the form of God, did not count equality with God a thing to be grasped, 7 but emptied himself, by taking the form of a servant, being born in the likeness of men. 8 And being found in human form, he **humbled** himself by becoming obedient to the point of death, even death on a cross. 9 Therefore God has highly **exalted** him and bestowed on him the name that is above every name, 10 so that at the name of Jesus every knee should bow, in heaven and on earth and under the earth, 11 and every tongue confess that Jesus Christ is Lord, to the glory of God the Father.

Colossians

3:15 (ESV) And let the peace of Christ rule in your hearts, to which indeed you were called in one body. And be thankful. 16 Let the word of Christ dwell in you richly, teaching and admonishing one another in all wisdom, singing psalms and hymns and spiritual songs, with thankfulness in your hearts to God. 17 And **whatever you do, in word or deed, do everything in the name of the Lord Jesus, giving thanks to God the Father through him.**

A good summary of the Christian life.

1 Thessalonians

5:16 (ESV) Rejoice always, 17 pray without ceasing, 18 give thanks in all circumstances; for this is the will of God in Christ Jesus for you. 19 Do not quench the Spirit. 20 Do not despise prophecies, 21 but test everything; hold fast what is good. 22 Abstain from every form of evil. 23 Now may the God of peace himself sanctify you completely, and may your whole spirit and soul and body be kept blameless at the coming of our Lord Jesus Christ. 24 **He who calls you is faithful; he will surely do it.**

I want to put my faith in Jesus but I don't know what to do. Jesus will show me the way.

2 Thessalonians

2:16 (ESV) Now may our Lord Jesus Christ himself, and God our Father, who loved us and gave us eternal comfort and good hope through grace, **comfort** your hearts and establish them in every good work and word.

Jesus is the source of comfort ... forever.

1 & 2 Timothy

1 Timothy 2:5 (ESV) For there is one God, and there is **one mediator** between God and men, the man **Christ Jesus**, 6 who **gave himself** as a **ransom** for all, which is the testimony given at the proper time.

I have often thought that I was not good enough for God to love.

The Letters

But Jesus has already taken care of that.

My commander, Jesus, wants me to tell others about Him.

Could it be that I won't know what I have until I share it with others? — even my relationship to Jesus?

When I feel alone, discouraged, or like quitting, I try to imagine Jesus and the crowd of those who have gone before me cheering me on.

Titus

1:1 (ESV) Paul, a servant of God and an apostle of Jesus Christ, for the sake of the faith of God's elect and their knowledge of the truth, which accords with godliness, 2 in hope of eternal life, which God, who never lies, promised before the ages began 3 and at the proper time manifested in his word through the preaching with which I have been entrusted by the **command of God our Savior.**

Philemon

1:4 (ESV) I thank my God always when I remember you in my prayers, 5 because I hear of your love and of the faith that you have toward the Lord Jesus and for all the saints, 6 and I pray that the **sharing of your faith** may become effective for the full knowledge of every good thing that is in us for the sake of Christ.

Hebrews

12:1 (ESV) Therefore, since **we are surrounded** by so great a cloud of witnesses, let us also lay aside every weight, and sin which clings so closely, and let us run with endurance the race that is set before us, 2 **looking to Jesus**, the founder and perfecter of our faith, who for the joy that was set before him endured the cross, despising the shame, and is seated at the right hand of the throne of God.

James

4:13 (ESV) Come now, you who say, "Today

or tomorrow we will go into such and such a town and spend a year there and trade and make a profit"— 14 yet you do not know what tomorrow will bring. What is your life? For you are a mist that appears for a little time and then vanishes. 15 Instead you ought to say, "*If the Lord wills*, we will live and do this or that."

1 Peter

1:3 (ESV) Blessed be the God and Father of our Lord Jesus Christ! According to his great mercy, he has caused us to be born again to a living hope through the resurrection of Jesus Christ from the dead, 4 to **an inheritance that is imperishable, undefiled, and unfading**, kept in heaven for you, 5 who by God's power are being guarded through faith for a salvation ready to be revealed in the last time. 6 In this you rejoice, though now for a little while, if necessary, you have been grieved by various trials, 7 so that the tested genuineness of your faith—more precious than gold that perishes though it is tested by fire—may be found to result in praise and glory and honor at the revelation of Jesus Christ. 8 Though you have not seen him, you love him. Though you do not now see him, you believe in him and rejoice with joy that is inexpressible and filled with glory, 9 obtaining the outcome of your faith, the salvation of your souls.

2 Peter

1:3 (ESV) His divine power has granted to us all things that pertain to life and godliness, through the knowledge of him who called us

---

People used to sign letters with D.V.—Deo Valente—which is Latin for "If the Lord wills."

Everything I own will one day fade, become defiled, and ultimately perish.

I will go through trials that will test my faith. But the hope given to me by the resurrection of Christ will guard my faith through it all.

The Letters

The tragedy of an ineffective life.

The trinity—the Father, the Son (Jesus), and the Holy Spirit. One God, three persons.

Amen!

to his own glory and excellence, 4 by which he has granted to us his precious and very great promises, so that through them you may become partakers of the divine nature, having escaped from the corruption that is in the world because of sinful desire. 5 For this very reason, make every effort to supplement your faith with virtue, and virtue with knowledge, 6 and knowledge with self-control, and self-control with steadfastness, and steadfastness with godliness, 7 and godliness with brotherly affection, and brotherly affection with love. 8 For if these qualities are yours and are increasing, they keep you from being **ineffective** or unfruitful in the knowledge of our Lord Jesus Christ.

1 & 2 & 3 John

1 John 4:13 (ESV) By this we know that we abide in him and he in us, because he has given us of his **Spirit**. 14 And we have seen and testify that the **Father** has sent his **Son** to be the Savior of the world. 15 Whoever confesses that Jesus is the Son of God, God abides in him, and he in God.

Jude

1:24 (ESV) Now to him who is able to keep you from stumbling and to present you blameless before the presence of his glory with great joy, 25 to the only God, our Savior, **through Jesus Christ our Lord**, be glory, majesty, dominion, and authority, before all time and now and forever. Amen.

9. The Book of Revelation

The Woman and the Dragon

12:12 (ESV) And a great sign appeared in heaven: a woman clothed with the sun, with the moon under her feet, and on her head a crown of twelve stars. 2 She was pregnant and was crying out in birth pains and the agony of giving birth. 3 And another sign appeared in heaven: behold, a great red dragon, with seven heads and ten horns, and on his heads seven diadems. 4 His tail swept down a third of the stars of heaven and cast them to the earth. And the dragon stood before the woman who was about to give birth, so that when she bore her child he might devour it. 5 She gave birth to a male child, one who is to rule all the nations with a rod of iron, but her child was caught up to God and to his throne, 6 and the woman fled into the wilderness, where she has a place prepared by God, in which she is to be nourished for 1,260 days.

Jesus is coming.

22:7 "Look, I am coming soon! Blessed are those who obey the words of prophecy written in this book. 16 "I, Jesus, have sent my angel to give you this message for the churches. I am both the source of David and the heir to his throne. I am the bright morning star."

17 The Spirit and the bride say, "Come." Let anyone who hears this say, "Come." Let anyone who is thirsty come. Let anyone who desires drink freely from the water of life. 18 And I solemnly declare to everyone

---

This story is an expanded version of what we read in Genesis. Gen. 3:15; pg. 107.

The woman represents Eve and then ultimately Mary (the mother of Jesus). The red dragon is the Devil. His goal was and is to stop God's plan of salvation through Jesus.

who hears the words of prophecy written in this book: If anyone adds anything to what is written here, God will add to that person the plagues described in this book. 19 And if anyone removes any of the words from this book of prophecy, God will remove that person's share in the tree of life and in the holy city that are described in this book.

20 He who is the faithful witness to all these things says, "**Yes, I am coming soon!**"

Amen! Come, Lord Jesus!

21 May the grace of the Lord Jesus be with God's holy people.

In my life time?

Thanks for reading the Jesus Bible. I hope you not only learned about Jesus but that you expereinced Him speaking to you. If you want to learn more, talk to the person who gave you this book or any church going, Bible believing Christian.